Practical Strategies
for
Improving Instruction

Karen D. Wood

NATIONAL MIDDLE SCHOOL ASSOCIATION

nmsa ®

NATIONAL MIDDLE SCHOOL ASSOCIATION

Karen Wood, a former middle school teacher and instructional coordinator, is a Professor at the University of North Carolina at Charlotte. Dr. Wood is nationally recognized in the field of reading and language arts and has published extensively, including her regular column in the *Middle School Journal,* "Out of Research—Into Practice."

NMSA is grateful to her for her service since 1986 as a column author and for her assistance in preparing this volume. Thanks also to Mary Mitchell for her work in designing and formatting the monograph.

ISBN 1-56090-082-2

*To Eric, Ryan, Kevin, and Lauren
as well as my imaginary friend.*

Contents

Strategies Organized by Categories

The following categories have been established to assist in selecting appropriate strategies. Several of the strategies address more than one instructional concern and appear, therefore, more than once.

Foreword

Middle level teachers are unique not just by virtue of who we teach but by how we teach. We emphasize strategies that actively engage students of all ability levels, promote collaboration, provide for various levels of concrete and abstract thought, and foster student inquiry.

Preparing today's students for tomorrow's challenges is of paramount importance to educators, parents, and the community itself. While this may seem like a vague, rhetorical generality, it is in fact a truth. For teachers in the classroom, then, their monumental task lies in deciding what can be taught that will have lasting value in years to come. As a middle level teacher, I both cherish and value the instructional time I have and seek activities that are not only interesting and fun but are directed toward valid objectives and reflect our knowledge of learning as research has shown it to be.

Assessing reading and writing, cooperative learning, vocabulary development, reading comprehension, and critical thinking are all basic topics of instructional concern for middle level teachers regardless of their subject matter specialty. This monograph provides sound, engaging approaches to these and other topics that are directly reflective of current research. The strategies provided, in toto, make a strong and significant contribution to the resources available to assist teachers in improving instruction in the ultimately important "learning to learn" part of our curriculum.

Busy teachers will appreciate *Practical Strategies for Improving Instruction* because it provides step-by-step procedures along with classroom examples in a convenient and serviceable format. This handbook should be a readily available resource for all middle level educators who are seeking to make a difference by ensuring success for all students.

Charlene Pike, 1993-94 President
National Middle School Association

Preface

This book provides teachers with a handbook of research-based teaching strategies that are applicable to all subject areas. These instructional approaches originally appeared as columns in the *Middle School Journal*. Each of the twenty-three strategies begins with a foundation in research findings and proceeds with practical implications for classroom use. Step-by-step procedures are given where appropriate along with classroom examples using actual instructional materials available in our schools.

The Introduction provides an overview of the research on prevailing versus preferred instructional practices in our middle schools and discusses what can be done to improve instruction in five basic areas: (1) approaches to teaching, (2) lesson planning and implementation, (3) classroom instructional resources, (4) instructional activities and arrangements, and (5) promotion of higher order thinking.

Strategies 1 and 2 are concerned with assessing the reading and writing performance of students to determine strengths and weaknesses in certain areas. Strategies 3 through 9 center around the topic of cooperative learning as it relates to various topics including writing, viewing, notetaking, oral reading, and subject area learning. The next four strategies (10 through 13) show practical ways to develop students' vocabulary with examples spanning all the curricular areas. The remaining strategies are on improving students' comprehension and appreciation of what they read including ways to make the reading of textbook material more meaningful, asking questions which enhance understanding, and using brainstorming to maximize participation and recall.

Improving instruction in the middle grades

In five basic areas of instruction research provides ample justification for changing current practices to more effective ones.

Throughout the years, much attention has been focused on the reorganizational dimensions of the middle school, what constitutes an exemplary middle school, as well as on characteristics of early adolescents themselves, who they are and what they are like. However, much less attention has been given to the most effective ways of teaching students at this level in dynamic, motivating, and developmentally appropriate ways.

While classroom research on middle grade instructional practices is sparse, Wood (1990) and Wood and Muth (1991) reviewed the existing literature and found a vast need for improvement in at least five areas of instruction: approaches to teaching; lesson planning and implementation; classroom instructional resources; instructional activities and assignments; and promotion of higher order thinking. Each of these five areas is discussed in terms of what research suggests is customary practice coupled with the indicated directions for improvement.

Approaches to Teaching

Customary practice: The lecture approach; more telling, mentioning, or assigning than actual teaching.

There is ample research to indicate that the lecture approach, wherein teachers do the majority of the talking and students sit and listen, continues to dominate (California State Department of Education, 1987; Carnegie Council on Adolescent Development, 1989; Cuban, 1984; Goodlad, 1984; Lounsbury & Johnston, 1985; Lounsbury and Clark, 1990). This classroom phenomenon exists despite evidence that other more effective means of communicating information which involve a continuous interaction between teacher and student are available.

Indicated directions: Collaborative learning, modeling, thinking aloud.

Rather than using the whole class lecture approach, middle grade teachers can structure their presentations in ways that allow students to participate in peer learning, helping, and information-seeking lessons. Research on collaborative learning dates back to the late 19th century with hundreds of studies conducted worldwide attesting to its many benefits. It has been demonstrated that collaborative learning not only aids the cognitive dimension of learning by increasing achievement test scores, but it also aids the affective dimension by helping students develop better relationships with one another, thereby increasing self-esteem (Glasser in Brandt, 1988; Johnson & Johnson, 1985; Lehr, 1984; Slavin, 1983).

Collaborative learning techniques such as group retellings, dyadic learning, research, interest, base or tutorial grouping can be motivating vehicles for communicating subject matter (Wood, 1987; see Strategies 3 through 9 for more ideas on collaborative learning). Another alternative approach is teacher modeling in which teachers directly demonstrate the processes, strategies, assignments, and techniques they want students to learn and apply to other situations independently. Modeling can be accomplished through the use of "think alouds" as described by Davey (1983) wherein the teacher makes the invisible thinking processes visible by talking aloud how to work through a particular learning task. Modeling can also be accomplished through the use of demonstrations, examples, and explanations as suggested by Roehler and Duffy (1981) and Blanton, Moorman, and Wood (1986).

Lesson Planning and Implementation

Customary practice: Looking up lists of definitions in the dictionary; assigning reading with no preparation, direction, or follow-up discussion.

Research indicates that the majority of instructional time is devoted to presenting information with little attention to instructional readiness (preparation for reading) and the internalization of concepts (Ratekin, Simpson, Alvermann, & Dishner, 1985; Smith & Feathers, 1983). In such instances, teachers may be observed merely telling students to open their textbooks and begin reading with little attention to background building, purpose for reading, or guidance. In addition, vocabulary instruction typically lacks depth of mental processing necessary to ensure learning and retention and frequently involves looking up definitions and assigning and testing lists of words (Irvin & Connors, 1989; Nagy, 1988;

Ratekin, Simpson, Alvermann, & Dishner, 1985; Smith & Feathers, 1983). Research also shows that little time is spent on helping students understand their classroom reading material in the way of content area reading strategies such as study guides, vocabulary guides, or graphic organizers (Irvin & Connors, 1989; Ratekin, Simpson, Alvermann, & Dishner, 1985; Smith & Feathers, 1983).

Indicated directions: Teaching with a sound instructional framework; helping students become strategic readers; meaningful vocabulary development strategies.

Teachers can assist students with the demands of subject area reading by teaching within a sound instructional framework including a pre-reading (or preparation) phase, a guided reading phase, and a post-reading (or follow up) phase (Readence, Bean, & Baldwin, 1989). And, when deemed appropriate, a model of direct instruction involving demonstrations, guided and independent practice may be used (Baumann, 1983; Pearson, 1985; Blanton, Moorman, & Wood, 1986). Within this instructional framework, teachers can build students' background and conceptual understanding by eliciting their prior knowledge on a topic before beginning the lesson.

Background information can be developed in a number of ways including guided imagery and visualization (see Strategy 12), brainstorming techniques such as Carr and Ogle's KWL Plus (1987) described in detail in Strategy 11, Taba's list (1967), group label and write and story impressions (see Strategy 7), as well as a variety of other teacher-directed pre-reading activities (Moore, Readence, & Rickelman, 1989).

Students can also be taught to be strategic readers who engage in mental modeling (Duffy, Roehler, & Herrmann, 1988), a kind of internal think-aloud process, and who engage in self-monitoring, a means of alerting themselves when a portion of text is misunderstood and requires rereading or outside assistance.

To further enhance students' conceptual understanding of subject matter, teachers can use vocabulary development strategies that involve deeper and richer processing and employ a combination of definition as well as context (see Strategies 10-14 for additional vocabulary strategies). The combination of explicit definition, rich contextual information, and ample student involvement and interaction with the new terms has been a proven means for developing and extending students' vocabulary knowledge (Nagy, 1988). Techniques such as semantic mapping (Heimlich & Pittelmann, 1986) and the vocabulary self-collection (Haggard, 1986), and preview-in-context strategies (Readence, Bean, & Baldwin, 1989) are highly recommended to meet these needs.

Classroom Instructional Resources

Customary practice: Over-reliance on textbooks, workbooks, and worksheets; single assignments for all students.

Research continues to show that the textbook is the primary instructional material to which middle grade students are exposed (EPIE, 1977; Goodlad, 1976;1984) despite the fact that these textbooks are often too difficult for them to read and comprehend(Armbruster&Anderson, 1981; Armbruster & Gudbrandsen, 1986; Cousins, 1989). Teachers tend to lecture and test on information presented in the textbook, leaving students with little incentive to read and learn from the textbooks on their own (Smith & Feathers, 1983; Ratekin, Simpson, Alvermann, & Dishner, 1985). These assignments often mean answering the end-of-chapter questions which accompany most textbooks and of-

ten do not adequately reflect the major concepts of the selection.

Along with the textbook, workbooks and worksheets tend to proliferate with teachers spending an abundance of class time monitoring independent seat work (Goodlad, 1984; Mitman, Mergendoller, Packer, & Marchman, 1984; Sanford, 1985) . In general, research suggests that innovative teaching and learning methods tend to be infrequent in middle grade classrooms (Goodlad, 1984; Eccles & Midgley, 1989; Lounsbury and Johnston, 1988; Lounsbury and Clark, 1990).

Indicated directions: Reducing the demands of printed material by using study guides, peer reading and retelling, collective recall and text structure strategies; use of multiple resources; media, technology, trade books, and original documents.

There is heavy documentation and support for the use of media and other technology coupled with the use of multiple resources such as trade books, field trips, and original documents (Aiex, 1988; California State Department of Education, 1987; Carnegie Council on Adolescent Development, 1989; Goodlad, 1984—see Strategy 9 for ways to use video tapes and other media). The use of multiple forms of media coupled with strategic use of the textbook and other forms of print can be a dynamic and motivating method of presenting content. The point is that textbooks need not be the sole purveyor of information second only to the teacher. Instead, textbooks can form the core of the instructional program on which other sources of information are based.

When textbooks are used, teachers can help students deal with the heavy reading demands by de-

"Innovative teaching and learning methods tend to be infrequent in middle grade classrooms"

veloping questions in the form of study guides which students can use as aids while reading (Wood, Lapp, & Flood, 1992). Such guided questions and activities serve as "tutors in print form" to assist students while they are reading the text, not to just interrogate them afterwards.

Some examples are the textbook activity guide (Davey, 1986), the point-of-view, and interactive guides (see Strategies 5, 18, 19 and 22 for examples of these guides). Teachers can also reduce the amount of print students must deal with at a given time by encouraging peer reading and re-telling (Wood, 1987) and by us-ing other collective recall strategies such as Manzo's (1975) guided reading procedure (described in Strategy 21) or one of the many strategies designed to help students understand how different types of texts are structured (Armbruster, Anderson, & Ostertag, 1989; Richgels, McGee, & Slaton, 1989).

> "Active, hands-on learning and the promotion of higher order thinking result in greater academic benefit."

motion of higher order thinking results in greater academic benefits (Anderson et al., 1985; California State Department of Education, 1987; Carnegie Council on Adolescent Development, 1989; Eccles & Midgley, 1989; Lipsitz, 1984). Students can engage in experiments in science classrooms working in groups to hypothesize about the outcome. They can select topics for further research in social studies and develop a model, recreate a scene, have a debate or visit an historical site. In language arts, students can be grouped for communal writing (see Strategy 12) to write their own plays, design travel brochures, or write a letter to a government official. In mathematics, they can learn how to apply their computational skills and formula knowledge to solve real life problems: constructing a building, making a purchase, or planning a trip. (See Strategy 14 for more ideas in mathematics.) In short, the literature abounds with new ideas for teaching and learning information which elicit students' critical thinking abilities and maximizes their involvement.

Instructional Activities and Assignments

Customary practice: Drill and practice exercises, extensive seat work, memorization of facts, literal level thinking.

According to a recent national survey, drill and practice exercises are often twice as frequent as reading and discussion in all subject area classrooms (Becker, 1990). In synthesizing the findings from other studies, it has also been found that students are expected to memorize a lot of facts, recite, recall, and engage in teacher assigned seat work (Goodlad, 1984; Rounds & Osaki, 1983; Sirotnik, 1983).

Indicated directions: Active, hands-on learning; higher-order thinking.

It has been widely established and recommended that active, hands-on learning and the pro-

Promotion of Higher Order Thinking

Customary practice: Abundance of literal level questions; factual recall tasks.

Studies have indicated that the majority of questions posed by teachers, especially at grade 7 and above, still tend to be literal recall (Johnston & Markle, 1986; Smith & Feathers, 1983; Stiggins et al., 1989). Likewise, the majority of questions presented in textbooks tend to require more detail than main idea response (Armbruster, 1984; Trachtenburg, 1974). Research has shown that critical thinking, considered a basic goal, is not taught extensively to-day (Johnston & Markle, 1986; Resnick, 1987).

Also, the need to show students how to relate new information to existing knowledge, integral to effective problem solving, is frequently overlooked (Johnston & Markle, 1986).

Indicated directions: Asking higher level questions; using statements instead of questions; small group problem solving sessions.

Research reveals that understanding is increased through higher level questions (Redfield & Rousseau, 1981; Wixson, 1983) as well as strategically developed statements (Dillon, 1982). In order to help students think beyond the literal level of the printed or oral information, teachers can develop questions requiring them to infer, synthesize information, and merge their own background knowledge with the content. Raphael's question-answer relationships or QAR's are one device for meeting this need. Students are taught what kinds of questions to look for as well as where to find the answer: on the page (textually explicit), on the page and in their head (textually implicit), or just in their own head (scriptally implicit). (See Strategy 20.)

One particularly effective approach for the promotion of critical thinking abilities which can be applied in all subject areas is the reaction guide (see Strategy 19). Students work in pairs or small groups to react to a series of generalized statements about a topic before and after reading the material.

A Final Note

The instructional practices delineated here, while not exhaustive, can be used to guide administrators or teachers as they engage in observational evaluations of their own or others' teaching performance. This review reveals that a wealth of dynamic instructional strategies exists in professional literature, and these strategies have the potential to make the middle years more richly rewarding, both cognitively and affectively, than ever before. ♞

References

Aiex, N.K. (1988). Using film, video, and TV in the classroom. *ERIC Digest, 11,* Bloomington, IN: Clearinghouse on Reading and Communication Skills, Indiana University.

Anderson, R.C., Hiebert, E.H., Scott, J.A., & Wilkinson, I.A.G. (1985). *Becoming a nation of readers: The report on the commission on reading.* Washington, DC: National Institute of Education, U.S. Department of Education.

Armbruster, B.B. (1984). The problem of "inconsiderate text." In G. Duffy, L. Roehler, & J. Mason (Eds.), *Comprehension instruction: Perspectives and suggestions.* New York: Longman.

Armbruster, B.B., & Anderson, T.H. (1981). *Content area textbooks.* Reading Education Report No. 23. Urbana, IL: Center for the Study of Reading, University of Illinois.

Armbruster, B.B., Anderson, T.H., & Ostertag, J. (1989). Teaching text structure to improve reading and writing. *Journal of Reading, 43,* 130-137.

Armbruster, B.B., & Gudbrandsen, B. (1986). Reading comprehension instruction in social studies programs. *Reading Research Quarterly, 21,* 36-48.

Baumann, J. (1983). A generic comprehension instructional strategy. *Reading World, 22,* 284-293.

Becker, H.J. (1990). Curriculum and instruction in middle-grade schools. *Kappan, 71,* 450-457.

Blanton, W.E., Moorman, G.B., & Wood, K.D. (1986). A model of direct instruction applied to the basal skills lesson. *The Reading Teacher, 40,* 299-305.

Brandt, R. (1988). On students' needs and team learning. A conversation with William Glasser. *Educational Leadership, 45,*(6), 38-45.

California State Department of Education. (1987). *Caught in the middle: Educational reform for young adolescents in California public schools.* Sacramento, CA: Author.

Carnegie Council on Adolescent Development. (1989). *Turning points: Preparing American youth for the 21st century.* Washington, DC: Carnegie Corporation.

Carr, D., & Ogle, D. (1987). K-W-L plus: A strategy in comprehension and summarization. *Journal of Reading, 30,* 626-631.

Cousins, P.T. (1989). Content area textbooks: Friends or foes? *ERIC Digest.* Bloomington, IN: Clearinghouse on Reading and Communication Skills, Indiana University.

Cuban, L. (1984). *How teachers taught: Constancy and change in American classrooms 1890-1980.* New York: Longman.

Davey, B. (1983).Think aloud—modeling the cognitive processes of reading comprehension. *Journal of Reading, 27,* 44-47.

Davey, B. (1986). Using textbook activity guides to help students learn from textbooks. *Journal of Reading, 29,* 489-494.

Dillon, J.T. (1982). Cognitive correspondence between question/statement and responses. *American Educational Research Journal, 19,* 540-551.

Duffy, G.G., Roehler, L.R., & Herrmann, B.A. (1988). Modeling mental processes helps poor readers become strategic readers. *The Reading Teacher, 41,* 762-767.

Eccles, J.S., & Midgley, C. (1989). Stage-environment fit: Developmentally appropriate classrooms for young adolescents. In C. Ames & R. Ames (Eds.), *Research on motivation in education, Volume 3, Goals and Cognitions.* New York: Academic Press.

Educational Products Information Exchange. (1977). *Report on national study of the nature and the quality of instructional materials most used by teachers and learners.* EPIE Report No. 17. Stonybrook, NY: EPIE Institute.

Goodlad, J.I. (1984). *A place called school.* New York: McGraw-Hill.

Goodlad, J.1.(1976). *Facing the future: Issues in education and schooling.* New York: McGraw-Hill.

Haggard, M.R. (1986). The vocabulary self-collection strategy: Using student interest and world knowledge to enhance vocabulary growth. *Journal of Reading, 29,* 634-642.

Heimlich, J., & Pittleman, S. (1986). *Semantic mapping: Classroom applications.* Newark, DE: International Reading Association.

Irvin, J.L., & Connors, N.A.(1989). Reading instruction in middle level schools: Results of a U.S. survey. *Journal of Reading, 32,* 306-311.

Johnson, R.T., & Johnson, D.W. (1985) . Student-student interaction: Ignored but powerful. *Journal of Teacher Education, 36,* 22-26.

Johnston, J.H., & Markle, G.C. (1986). *What research says to the middle level practitioner.* Columbus, OH: National Middle School Association.

Lehr, F. (1984). Cooperative learning. *Journal of Reading, 27,* 458-460.

Lipsitz, J. (1984). *Successful schools for young adolescents.* Brunswick, NJ: Transaction Books.

Lounsbury, J.H., & Clark, D.C. (1990). *Inside grade eight: From apathy to excitement.* Reston, VA: National Association of Secondary School Principals.

Lounsbury, J.H., & Johnston, J.H. (1985). *How fares the ninth grade?* Reston, VA: National Association of Secondary School Principals.

Lounsbury, J.H. & Johnston, J.H. (1988). *Life in the three sixth grades.* Reston, VA: National Association of Secondary School Principals.

Manzo, A.V. (1975). Guided reading procedure. *Journal of Reading, 28,* 287-291.

Mitman, A.L., Mergendoller, J.R., Packer, M.J., & Marchman, V.A. (1984). *Scientific literacy in seventh grade life science: A study of instructional process, task completion, student perceptions and learning outcomes: Final report.* San Francisco, CA: Far West Laboratory.

Moore, D.W., Readence, J.E., & Rickelman, R.J. (1989). *Prereading activities for content area reading and learning.* (2nd ed.). Newark, DE: International Reading Association.

Nagy, W.E. (1988). *Teaching vocabulary to improve reading comprehension.* NCTE/IRA.

Pearson, P.D. (1985). Changing the face of reading comprehension instruction. *The Reading Teacher, 30,* 724-738.

Ratekin, N., Simpson, M.L., Alvermann, D.E., & Dishner, E.K. (1985). Why teachers resist content reading instruction. *Journal of Reading, 28,* 432-437.

Readence, J.E., Bean, T.W., & Baldwin, R.S. (1989). *Content area reading: An integrated approach.* Dubuque, IA: Kendall-Hunt.

Redfield, D.L., & Rousseau, E.W. (1981). A metaanalysis of the experimental research on teacher questioning behavior. *Review of Educational Research, 51,* 237-245.

Resnick, L.B. (1987). *Education and learning to think report.* Washington, DC: National Academy Press.

Richgels, D.J., McGee, L.M., & Slaton, E.A. (1989). Teaching expository text structure in reading and writing. In K.D. Muth (Ed.), *Children's comprehension of text* (pp. 167-184). Newark, DE: International Reading Association.

Roehler, L.R., & Duffy, G .G. (1984). Direct explanation of comprehension processes. In G.G. Duffy, L.R. Roehler, and J. Mason (Eds.), *Comprehension instruction: Perspectives and suggestions.* New York: Longman.

Rounds, T.S., & Osaki, S.Y. (1983). *The social organization of classrooms: An analysis of sixth and seventh grade activity structures* (Report EPSSP-82-5) San Francisco, CA: Far West Laboratory.

Sanford, J.P. (1985). *Comprehension-level tasks in secondary classrooms* (R & D Rep. No. 6199), Austin, TX: Research and Development Center for Teacher Education, University of Texas at Austin.

Sirotnik, K.A. (1983). What you see is what you get—consistency, persistency, and mediocrity in classrooms. *Harvard Educational Review, 53*(1), 16-31.

Slavin, R.E. (1983). *Cooperative learning.* New York: Longman.

Smith,F.R., & Feathers,K.M. (1983). The role of reading in content classrooms: Assumption vs. reality. *Journal of Reading, 27,* 262-267.

Stiggins, R., Griswold, M., & Wikelund, K. (1989). Measuring thinking skills through classroom assessment. *Journal of Educational Measurement, 26,* 233-246.

Taba, H. (1967). *Teacher's handbook for elementary social studies reading.* Boston, MA: Addison-Wesley.

Trachtenburg, D. (1974). Student tasks and test materials: What cognitive skills do they tap? *Peabody Journal of Education, 52,* 54-57.

Wixson, K. (1983). Questions about a text: What you ask about is what children learn. *The Reading Teacher, 37,* 287-293.

Wood, K.D. (1987). Fostering cooperative learning in middle and secondary level classrooms. *Journal of Reading, 31,* 10-18.

Wood, K.D. (1990). Prevailing versus preferred instructional practices in the middle grades. Paper presented at the meeting of the International Reading Association, Atlanta, GA.

Wood, K.D., Lapp, D., & Flood, J. (1992). *Guiding readers through text: A review of study guides.* Newark, DE: International Reading Association.

Wood, K.D., & Muth, K.D. (1991, October). The case for improved instruction in the middle grades. *Journal of Reading 35,* 84-90.

To declare oneself against the institution of the three Rs in the schools is like being against motherhood or the flag. Beyond question, students ought to be literate and ought to revel in their literacy. Yet the essential emptiness of this goal is dramatized by the fact that young children in the United States are becoming literate in a *literal* sense; that is, they are mastering the rules of reading and writing, even as they are learning their addition and multiplication tables. What is missing are not the decoding skills, but two other facets: the capacity to read for understanding and the desire to read at all. Much the same story can be told for the remaining literacies; it is not the mechanics of writing nor the algorithms for subtraction that are absent, but rather the knowledge about when to invoke these skills and the inclination to do so productively in one's own daily life.

—Howard Gardner
The Unschooled Mind: How Children Think and How Schools Should Teach

How to assess writing performance across the curriculum

Described are three modes of grading students' writing performance including teacher, peer, and self-assessment.

The process approach to writing, which emerged in the seventies, is largely responsible for revolutionizing the teaching of writing and making the educational community aware that instructional changes were needed (Harp & Brewer, 1991; Tompkins, 1990). In the process approach, writers move recursively through a series of teacher-modeled stages: prewriting, drafting, revisions, editing and sharing (Atwell, 1987; Calkins, 1986; Graves, 1987). Unlike traditional approaches in which students were first taught the mechanics of writing (grammar, punctuation, and spelling), students involved in process writing are given the freedom to put their ideas in print to be polished and refined in subsequent drafts. The theory is that students learn how to write by writing—everyday—using diverse styles and topics.

Yet, what middle level teacher has time to grade all of these compositions? Process writing advocates emphatically recommend that it is not necessary to grade every written product. Many writing assignments must be considered practice efforts engaged in for the purpose of self-improvement. Just as the neophyte bike rider must practice individually before displaying the newly attained talent for parental approval, the neophyte writer (and adolescents are still very new to many writing trials) must be allowed several trails before risking the ultimate judgment by the teacher.

When the teacher feels it is necessary to finalize a first draft or turn a paper in for credit, a number of assessment strategies can be employed. Examples of strategies in three areas: teacher assessment, peer assessment, and self-assessment. are described below.

Teacher Assessment

Checkpoint scales

Kirby and Liner (1981) have devised a writing assessment strategy called checkpoint scales. Teachers can develop the criteria for checkpoint scales to coordinate with specific curricular objectives, making the scale reflect subject area content and/or technical objectives (e.g., grammar, punctuation, coherence, etc.). Students' scores on each criteria are multiplied by a number (listed at the end of the line in the example) depending upon how much weight is allotted to each element. As illustrated, an element listed on this scale is "Overall Impression" which provides a general opinion of the composition similar to holistic scoring. An overall numerical grade and comments are given for each paper to allow the student to locate, revise, and repair any areas of need.

Checkpoint Scales

Name *Ryan*
Date *February 14*
Grade *8*

Your revised draft on *Descriptive writing*
"My room and what's in it."
received the following rating:

Organization (beginning, middle, and end)

1	2	③	4	5	X4=*12*
I had a lot of trouble following your plan. Rethink your outline and try to tighten this up.		You're on the right track, but it's still hard to follow your plan.		Great organization. I was right with you.	

Details (reasons, elaboration)

1	2	3	4	⑤	X4=*20*
You didn't give enough information. Be more specific but stay away from lists.		There are some good ideas here. You need to tell your reader a little more.		Good vivid details. I get the picture.	

Mechanics (proofing)

1	②	3	4	5	X3=*6*
Can't tell what you're trying to say with all the errors. Try again.		A few errors got by you this time. See if you can find them.		What a proofreader! You really have an eye for that job.	

Overall Impression

1	2	3	④	5	X5 *20*
You could do much more with this assignment. Return to the prewriting outline and start again.		The potential is there. With a little more effort you'll have it.		What a pleasure to read. You composed a fine piece of writing.	TOTAL=*58*

Comments:

Ryan, you are such a creative thinker. I love your descriptions! Rework that last paragraph. I had trouble following your ideas in the end. Also, be sure to proofread (especially punctuations). After that, you'll have a great composition.

Peer Assessment

Determining groups

Peer editing is a time-saving way to evaluate writing assessment by involving students in the process as well. Students can learn from both the writing and the editing process as they analyze their drafts for needed revisions in content and mechanics. Teachers can engage students in the peer editing process by asking that they choose a partner or by preassigning them to partners or small groups. The latter approach is often more effective because the teacher can group students according to similarities or differences in abilities, needs, or interests. Grouping students heterogeneously is beneficial because it allows students of all ranges to work together and contribute to the process in whatever way is most appropriate to their level.

Roles can be explained ahead of time so that each group member knows the specific task they must undertake. Harp and Brewer (1991) recommend the following instructional sequence for peer editing groups adding that teachers freely modify it for their own purposes.

Members take turns reading aloud their compositions to the group.

After each composition is read aloud, group members name at least one thing they liked about the manuscript. They must also make one or more suggestions for improvement. For example, "I really got excited when you described the ghost, but before that, it dragged a little. Maybe you could start with your second paragraph and leave off the first details."

The student author makes notes from the group members' comments for later revision. Two members of the group exchange papers and read the composition for changes in punctuation, grammar, and/or spelling.

The teacher will need to model the kinds of things students can look for and say when they are critiquing another's paper (Step 2). This can be done by displaying on an overhead or reading aloud a teacher-developed example which needs revision and then "talking aloud" with the aid of the class the strengths and weaknesses.

Scan scoring

Scan scoring is an assessment technique which begins with peer editing and culminates with the teacher's evaluative comments (described by Wood, 1987). The peer editing form for "Point of View" writing can be used generically in any subject area. The criteria to be examined can also be changed to coordinate with the writing assignment and specific class objectives.

In scan scoring, students are preassigned to groups of 4 or 5 and are given a specific role in the group. The role assignments can be determined by the teacher or by group members. The compositions of each group member are circulated, read, and evaluated with each member responsible for a par-

---

Peer Editing Form

Point of View
(Type of writing)

"Let's Save the Animals"
(Assignment Title)

Name *Kevin M.*
Date *November 30*
Class *Mrs. Spear*
Grade *7*

- -

Author   *Kevin M.*

Editor *Ryan*
Criteria *Beginning*

Telling about the pandas and dolphins first was a good idea. It made me want to help right away.

- -

Author   *Kevin M.*

Editor *Myron*
Criteria *Middle/End*

The middle is hard to understand, but the ending is pretty good.

- -

Author   *Kevin M.*

Editor *Mandy*
Criteria *Run-on sentences/
fragments*

Look at the middle paragraph. I think you have some sentence fragments.

- -

Author   *Kevin M.*

Editor *Sarah Ann*
Criteria *Spelling*

I circled the spelling errors I noticed.

ticular area. As illustrated, each member in this group reads the paper for one of the following: beginning, middle, end, run-on sentences, sentence fragments, or spelling.

The teacher may choose to have students revise their drafts at this stage according to the comments of their peers or have them turned in for further teacher evaluation. Using the Scoring Form below, the teacher elected to scan the compositions and peer editing responses first before asking the students to make revisions. The grading scale can also be modified to coordinate with teacher expectations and goals.

Self-assessment

Writing advocates routinely recommend the use of self-evaluation measures for classroom use (Atwell; 1987, Costello, 1992; Tompkins, 1990). Having students assess their own writing helps develop in-

dependence and self-reliance. Self-assessment can be conducted in rough drafts or completed composition stage. Tompkins (1990) recommends a checklist for students to use in assessing the quality of their rewriting and to determine whether they have met the requirements set forth by the teacher . A checklist such as the one on p. 12 can be mimeographed or written on the board or an overhead transparency. The boldface words will need to be reviewed or retaught to insure that the students fully understand the elements to be included. While shown here for use with a composition on a country (modified from Tompkins, 1990), the checklist can be adapted for many diverse topics, subject areas, grade, and ability levels.

Self-evaluation: Mechanics

The second student self-evaluation form shown on p. 12 emphasizes the mechanics of writing

---

Teacher Scoring Form

Score results for:
Point of view
"Let's Save the Animals"

(Assignment Title)

Name *Kevin Michaels*
Date *December 2*
Class *Language Arts/Social Studies*
Grade *7*

Content Criteria
good beginning
middle needs work
good ending

Proofing Criteria

sentence fragments
spelling

Grade Scale

A = all 3 content criteria and no proofing errors
B = all 3 content criteria with proofing errors
C = two of the three content criteria, no proofing errors

D = two of the three content areas with proofing errors
E = not enough content for assignment credit

Initial Grade   *B*   Final Grade _____

Comments: *Kevin, your beginning and ending convinced me to save the animals. The middle paragraphs are confusing. Clear up those 2 spelling errors and you'll have an A+ paper.*

Self-evaluation: Content
(modified from Tompkins, 1990)

Name *Lauren*   **Country** *Spain*

After writing your draft be certain you have included the following information:

Yes	No	
✔		Have you written information about the **geography** of the country?
	✔	Have you drawn a **map** of the country?
✔		Have you written information about the **history** of the country?
✔		Have you described the **topography** of the country?
	✔	Have you written information about the **economy** of the country?
✔		Have you written information about the **natural resources** of the country?
✔		Have you written information about the **climate** of your country?
✔		Have you written **something special** about the country?
✔		Have you included information that you **requested** about your country?

Briefly tell what your project plans are:

I plan on doing a skit with Kevin, Ryan, and Sarah Ann on bullfighting. Then I will have the class share their opinions in a panel discussion.

Self-evaluation: Mechanics

Name *Lauren*   Assignment *Summary Writing*
Date *January 24*   *"My Science Project on Pollution"*
                  Teacher *Mrs. Query*

A. Content
- ✔   Does it make sense?
- ✔   Did I use new words relating to the topic?
- *N/A*   Did I use interesting words to help the reader "picture" what I wrote?
- ⊖   Did I keep to the topic?

B. Sentence and Paragraph Structure
- ✔   Did I use capital letters at the beginning of each sentence and for proper nouns?
- ✔   Did I end each sentence with the correct punctuation?
- ⊖   Did I write complete sentences?
- ⊖   Did I use commas, apostrophes, quotation marks, and other punctuation correctly?
- ⊖   Did I have any run-on sentences?
- ⊖   Did I spell each word correctly?
- ⊖   Did I indent the first word of each paragraph?

C. Handwriting
- ✔   Did I write this in my best handwriting?

whereas the checklist is more concerned with the content of the written product. Teachers can, of course, revise and combine the two into one form or use each one separately to focus on specific lesson goals. The mechanics checklist draws students' attention to individual errors and encourages more careful proofreading of written assignments (Wood, 1987). Here, the students are required to indicate the area in need of repair with a minus and then circle it after making the corrections.

Summary

When writing is viewed as one of the communication processes, teachers are able to focus more on the writing process students use than on the product students develop. There is no better way to thwart the enthusiasm of a neophyte writer than by marking each paragraph with red ink. Fortunately, the days of counting the errors in a piece of writing have long since been replaced with new approaches which view writers as newcomers to this dimension of literacy whose ideas can only be respected and refined if they first get put on paper. ♞

References

Atwell, N. (1987). *In the middle: Writing, reading, and learning with adolescents.* Portsmouth, NH: Heinemann.

Calkins, L. (1986). *The art of teaching writing.* Portsmouth, NH: Heinemann.

Costello, M. (1992, May). The short story: Composition and editing. *Writing Teacher,* 35-37.

Graves, D. (1983). *Writing: Teachers and children.at work.* Portsmouth, NH: Heinemann.

Harp, B., & Brewer, J. A. (1991). *Reading and writing: Teaching for the connections.* New York: Harcourt, Brace, Jovanovich.

Kirby, D., & Liner, T. (1981). *Inside out: Developmental strategies for teaching writing.* Montclair, NJ: Boynton/Cook.

Tompkins, G. E. (1990). *Teaching writing: Balancing process and product.* Columbus, OH: Merrill.

Wood, K. D. (1987). Evaluating progress in the language arts. In C. R Personke and D. D. Johnson (Eds.), *Language arts instruction and the beginning teacher* (pp. 330-332). Englewood Cliffs, NJ: Prentice-Hall.

It is more important to know where you are going than to get there quickly. Do not mistake activity for achievement.

—Mabel Newcomber

Even a gem, without polishing, will not glitter.

—Ancient Proverb

How to determine if inability is the cause of low performance

The use of a content inventory can help to distinguish between inability and indolence.

Mark rushes through his work just so he can bother other students, throw paper, and joke with friends. He turns in math assignments which are not only sloppy but contain numerous errors. When asked to redo the work, he does so compliantly, but his second try is little improved from the original. His score on the first math test was 70.

Jennifer has just begun to notice boys. She loves to socialize and pass notes to fellow students. She comes from a middle class family who regularly attend school functions. While her verbal skills are adequate, her written work is below average. Jennifer's scores on the first test in science and social studies were 74 and 76 respectively.

If these scenarios sound familiar, then, like many of your fellow teachers, you are pondering over the cause of poor classroom performance. Is it indolence or inability? When indolence is implicated, the student has the ability to do the work, but simply chooses not to put forth the effort. When inability is the cause, the student actually lacks the requisite skills to complete the assignments and will likely need specialized assistance.

Such a determination needs to be made early in the year so teachers can make adjustments in as-

signments or approaches necessary. What resources are available for making this decision? Traditional teacher-made tests give no clues as to the cause; they only reflect the symptoms. Standardized tests are not sufficiently sensitive to the specific tasks in subject area classrooms, and furthermore, scores are often not available until well into the first semester. Listening to reports from former teachers is unreliable since students often perform differently given a change in teacher and subject matter.

Instead, a more efficient means of determining who will have difficulty handling the assignments for the course is through the use of a *content inventory*. (See Rakes and McWilliams, 1986; Readence, Bean and Baldwin, 1985; Shepherd, 1978 for examples.) The content inventory is a teacher-made diagnostic test administered to the class as a group during the first week of school. It is developed on the subject area textbook used in any course and is designed to assess student abilities in various areas. Some suggested categories for the inventory follow.

Knowledge of resources—The students respond to questions concerning their knowledge of library aids. Teachers can determine what abilities are necessary for completing major course requirements such as researching a chosen topic in social studies or seeking information about a scientific question. This section does not require the use of the textbook.

Traditional teacher made tests only reflect the symptoms.

Parts of the book—Students use their books to demonstrate knowledge of the table of contents, index, glossary, summary paragraphs, and footnotes. Many times it is assumed that middle level students already know how to make optimal use of textbook aids. However, research has demonstrated that middle level students reading on or below grade level experience much confusion regarding the underlying function of textbook aids. This is especially true since students at this level may be expected to read as many as eight different textbooks throughout the school year.

Vocabulary—Questions can be asked to determine the students' general knowledge of the prefixes, suffixes, and roots common to a specific content area. (e.g. anti-, pro- in Social Studies, micro-, macro-, bio- in Science). Specific words can be noted from the text to determine if the students can use context clues to arrive at the meaning.

Comprehension—The teacher prepares the student for reading a short selection by setting purposes and establishing background. Both literal and inferential questions are asked to determine the extent to which the students understand the content of the passage. This section will give teachers insights into students' abilities to effectively undertake typical textbook assignments such as answering end-of-the chapter questions.

Graphic aids—(maps, pictures, diagrams and graphs) Ask students what they do when encountering a map or graph in their textbooks and they will likely respond that they "skip it." Since the ability to interpret graphic aids is considered a functional reading skill often measured on statewide competency tests,

it is imperative that teachers and students alike give this area its due emphasis. Therefore, students are asked to refer to specific pages in their book to determine their knowledge and ability to interpret charts, maps, graphs, and processes.

The categories identified are merely suggestions and are dependent on both subject matter and course objectives. In math, for example, some categories might be "Knowing the Meaning of Symbols" (e.g. $<$, $>X\pm$ etc.), "Translating Words to Symbols" (e.g. The line containing points A and B is parallel to the line containing the points C and D; answer: m AB=mCD); "Understanding Vocabulary" (e.g., What is a midpoint? Draw an equilateral triangle.); and, of course, "Obtaining Information from Maps, Charts, and Graphs," to name a few. A sample inventory developed on a sixth grade social studies textbook follows.

Guidelines For Developing and Using A Content Inventory

Developing the inventory

First, examine your book and course objectives and develop categories which are representative of the major skills needed to be successful in your course. Develop five or more questions for each of the categories chosen.

Second, to determine if students can effectively read and comprehend the textbook for the course, design questions for the comprehension section around a short selection of approximately three pages. (It is often best to choose a selection from the beginning of the text before the material gets too technical).

Third, type the inventory on a master so that copies can be made for an entire class. Since most textbooks are adopted for five years or more, the inventory can be reused. In addition, inventories can be developed for other alternative materials used in the classroom.

Content Inventory
Sixth Grade Social Studies
Nations of the World
Macmillan Publishing Co. Inc., 1982

Directions: In most instances, you will use your book to answer the following questions. In some cases, you will be asked to draw upon your general knowledge of social studies. Remember, this is **not** a test and will not count as a grade. Instead, it is a way for me to determine how best to meet your needs. Do your very best but don't worry if you do not know some answers.

I. Knowledge of Resources
1. What is a biography? an autobiography?
2. What library aid should be used to find out what resources are available on "Indochina?"
3. If asked to do a research report on Napoleon Bonaparte, what resources would you use?
4. Name a set of encyclopedias. Tell how the topics are arranged.
5. If asked to do a report in class in which most of the information could be found in a magazine, what guide would tell you what magazine and issue to locate?

II. Parts of the Book
1. In which chapter would you find information about Luxembourg?
2. If you were asked to define the word *cuneiform,* where could you look first?
3. What pages in the book would you look to find information about "aqueducts?" What textbook aid is used for this purpose?
4. Look at the "Unit Preview" that precedes each unit. How does this help you in your study?
5. On what page would you look to find a diagram of how silk was made? What textbook aid did you use?

III. Vocabulary
1. Read the last paragraph in the first column on page 139. What are "junks?"
2. Read the first column on page 135. What is meant by the "open-door policy?"
3. What does the prefix "anti-" mean?
4. Using your own background knowledge, define the following:
   monsoon   gondola   equator   nomad   guerilla
5. Read the bottom of page 87 and describe an "obelisk" in your own words.

IV. Comprehension: Read pages 29-32 and answer the following questions:
1. How long ago did man begin using fire?
2. Explain the kind of rock which is best used for cutting.
3. In what ways did early man's life-style change when they began to raise animals?
5. Give some reasons why the number of people increased after the Ice Age.

V. Use of Maps, Charts, Diagrams, and Graphs
1. Refer to the maps on pages 538 and 539. What changes took place in Africa from 1924-1968?
2. Look at the graph on page 156. How many passenger cars were owned in Japan in 1976? How many television sets were owned in 1973?
3. The diagram on page 124 tells how natural rubber is made. From what source do we get rubber? Briefly describe the first three steps.
4. According to the product map on page 111, what area of India produces tea? Turn to the bar graph on page 332.
5. Which country is the world's third largest producer of cheese? How many times greater is cheese production in the Soviet Union versus that of Italy?

Administering the inventory

Administer the inventory to the class during the first week of school. It is extremely important to explain to the class that this is an inventory of their skills for this class, not a test to count as a grade for the course. An upbeat explanation should eliminate anxiety or any need to collaborate on the answers.

Go over the inventory and explain its components while they have a copy in hand. It may be helpful to read the questions orally before having the students complete the inventory.

Allow students to use their textbook for most of the answers since one of the major purposes of the inventory is to ascertain their ability to successfully handle the textbook intended for the course.

Scoring the inventory

The inventory can be evaluated according to the following criteria:

—90% or above correct: These students are reading the textbook at their instructional level suggesting that with teacher guidance in the form of study guides, pre-reading activities, demonstrations and explanations, the students should be able to benefit from instruction with this text.

—70 % or below: Students scoring in this range are reading the text on their **frustration level** and will likely experience much difficulty handling the textbook. Often, recall is sketchy, identification of some requisite concepts and book handling skills are unsatisfactory. Such students will need to be carefully observed doing other tasks to determine if similar results are noted and if additional testing is needed. Students reading the course textbook at frustration level will likely need alternative materials, specialized assignments, or at least extensive textbook modification strategies (e.g. study guides) used under varied classroom conditions (e.g. tutorial assistance or group work).

A profile can be developed for each class which indicates strengths and weaknesses for individual students and for the class as a group. Then, if a majority of students miss several items in a given area, for example, "Maps, Charts and Graphs," the teacher may choose to revise course objectives making certain to give those areas extra emphasis or group the students accordingly and provide additional assistance.

A classroom profile which might accompany the social studies inventory displayed previously is provided (p. 18). Examining the profile horizontally, the scores of Ho Then, and Millicent clearly suggest that they may be unable to handle individual assignments from the textbook. Stewart's borderline score and "restless" behavior warrant further observation. It may be that he has a disability which would require input from a resource specialist.

Tracie, Eric, and Bart, and possibly Kelly appear to be exceptional students who may require challenging and motivating assignments to maintain their interests. Apparently, Eric and Bart will have to be watched carefully and changes made to remedy their tendency to socialize. It appears that the remaining students will be reading the text on their instructional level, thereby benefiting from teacher guidance and explanation. Should any of the students scoring at the instructional level and especially the independent level perform poorly on subsequent classroom tests and assignments, it can be presumed that some other cause than lack of ability may be responsible. Students scoring at the frustration level on the inventory will clearly need adjustments made in their assignments, materials, and tests in order to maximize success and avert poor performance.

Examining the profile vertically, it is obvious that the major emphasis for this particular class should be on vocabulary and inferential comprehension. At some point, the teacher may group those students who received minuses in the "Knowledge of Resources" section for a review of library usage and terminology.

Summary

The purpose of the content inventory is two-fold: 1) to determine who can and who cannot benefit from instruction in the subject area textbook and 2) it makes it possible at the start of the year to distinguish between inability and other causes for low performance. As with any evaluation device, the content inventory should not be the sole criterion used.

Observing students' work, having students read a short selection and retell it in their own words, and providing alternative assignments on varied levels are needed to achieve a complete picture when students' performance is in question. This ongoing diagnosis and evaluation or more appropriately, "hypothesis-testing," is not just for use in September, but may be used throughout the school year. 🐎

CLASSROOM PROFILE

SUBJECT: Social Studies   PERIOD 6

GRADE: 6   DATE: September 2

Name	I. Knowledge of Resources	II. Parts of Book	III. Vocabulary	IV. Comprehension a. Literal	b. Inferential	V. Graphic Aids	Total Score	Comments
Kelly	–	+	–	+	+	+	87	
Ho Then	–	–	–	–	–	+	50	ESL student, attempted, responded well to help
Tery	–	+	–	+	–	+	78	
Whitman	+	+	–	+	–	+	75	
Mike	+	+	+	+	–	–	85	
Tracie	+	+	–	+	+	+	90	
Betsy	+	+	–	+	–	+	82	
Ryan	–	+	+	+	+	–	80	
Millicent	–	–	–	+	–	+	63	
Stewart	–	–	–	+	–	+	70	restless, wouldn't stay in seat
Eric	+	+	+	+	+	–	95	socializing with one another
Bart	+	+	–	+	+	+	95	socializing with one another

How to meet the social needs of adolescents through cooperative learning

Allowing students to work together in groups or pairs capitalizes on their strong need to interact socially.

The professional literature abounds with calls for less individual learning and more cooperative learning arrangements (Doda, George, McEwin, 1987; Lounsbury, 1985, Nickolai-Mays and Goetsch, 1986). Frequently, the rationale cited in these articles surrounds the social needs of adolescents.

In a report from a series of conferences on adolescent development funded by the Ford Foundation and other agencies (Lipsitz, 1979), participants recommended that institutions can best meet the needs of young adolescents by fostering peer interaction. Specifically the report stated that "Schools should provide an opportunity for peer and community interaction. Youth educating other youth should be encouraged. Ethnic and cultural identities should be emphasized (p. 49)."

Despite this theoretical emphasis, classroom observational research indicates that the lecture method, wherein the teacher is the primary purveyor of information and the students the passive recipients, continues to predominate in our schools today (Cuban, 1984; Goodlad, 1984; Ratekin et al. 1985, Lounsbury and Johnston, 1985). When the lecture method is employed, the social and physical needs of adolescents are ignored. Instead, students sit in straight rows, often assigned seats, with little oppor-

tunity to share an idea with a friend or discuss a newly learned concept.

Often accompanying the lecture method are directives such as: "Do your own work," "Stay in your seat," and "Be quiet." Lounsbury (1985) comments that these directives ought to be used more sparingly and only under testing situations. He further suggests that as social beings, adolescents will resort to whispering and even writing notes in order to meet their need to communicate with others.

The social needs of students are greatest between the ages of eleven and fifteen. During these years, a sense of acceptance and a need to belong to a group is at variance with the need to be recognized as a unique individual (George, 1982). Small group situations address these conflicting needs by providing an atmosphere for self-expression less threatening than the "risk-taking" that occurs when an individual speaks to an entire class.

Unless teachers have a variety of grouping techniques from which to choose, the employment of any one technique can become as ineffective and unmotivating as sole reliance on the lecture method. Therefore, a variety of cooperative learning arrangements that are easily implemented and appropriate for all subject areas are described (Wood, 1987).

Group retellings

One method for ensuring classwide participation is through the use of group retellings. In this approach students work in pairs or in groups of three or more with each member reading a different type of topically-related material. For example, a science or health teacher might select three varied selections on the topic of the cardiovascular system. One piece of material might be a brochure from the local health department on recognizing a heart attack; another could be an excerpt from an encyclopedia, and yet another an article from a magazine or newspaper. Each student in the group reads his or her piece and is responsible for retelling it in his or her own words to other group members who may interject with related information from their own readings or past experiences. In addition, one way to individualize this group activity is to assign the shorter, easier material to the less able students.

Buddy system

The buddy system approach (Fader, 1976), as the name implies, involves grouping students of varied abilities together and making them responsible for each other's learning. In this approach, before turning in any assignment, buddy system group members must check each other's work and offer assistance.

Fader suggests rearranging the class role from the "most prepared" for this class to the "least prepared." In a hypothetical class of 30 students, this list would be divided into thirds. Then, the top student from each of the-three divisions would work together; next, the number 2 students from each division, the number 3 students and so on until the last group would be composed of the last member of each of the three divisions.

What results are 10 heterogeneous groups of three students in which the differences in ability levels are minimized to avoid both boredom and intimidation. Yet, the differences are still sufficient to

ensure that they all can benefit from each other's experiences.

Research grouping

At any stage of the instructional lesson, before, during, or after the reading, students can work in groups to investigate an issue in more depth. Whether the choice is laboratory research involving actual scientific experiments or library research for the purpose of solving unanswered questions, research grouping is an excellent method to employ. For example, a social studies class may be divided into groups to gather more information on Civil War battles, generals, or everyday life. Or groups in a health class may seek varied sources to find more information on poison control or childhood diseases.

When employing research grouping, it is helpful to give students a collaborative sequence to follow with roles and tasks assigned to each group member. The sequence might begin with students in each group taking on the responsibility of searching varied sources, either encyclopedias, books, pamphlets or magazines for information on a topic. Then, one student can serve as a recorder while the group decides how to synthesize the sources. Next, a rough draft can be compiled with group members editing where necessary. (Any subsequent drafts can be written by a different recorder.) Finally, group members become editors, reading the paper for mechanical and content modifications. The illustration (p. 21) shows how this process can be depicted in abbreviated format to aid groups in understanding their roles and meeting their objectives. Ideally, this sequence, or one similar, should be written on the board and explained thoroughly prior to the lesson.

Cybernetic sessions

Maztal (1986) developed cybernetic sessions in which small groups of students respond to predetermined questions during a specified period of time. Cybernetic sessions can be used before a new lesson as a means of eliciting students' prior experiences with a topic. Or, they can be used after a lesson as a form of review. The four phases of cybernetic sessions will be described next.

Research Group Assignments

Each member: Assign research roles—encyclopedia, magazines, card catalog
Entire group: Combines notes
Individual: Rough draft recorder
Entire group: Read and revise
Individual: Second draft recorder
Each member: Assign editorial roles—grammar, punctuation, content
Entire group: Final copy reading and revision.

Preplanning Phase—Begin by writing one question on poster board and hanging the boards around the classroom. Some questions can be developed for science on the digestive system; in literature on the setting, problem resolution or characters in a novel; or in mathematics on everyday uses of the decimal system. Regardless of the subject area, the questions should be thought-provoking, eliciting much discussion and interaction.

Response Generating Phase—Students are assigned to groups of four to six and are then seated around each of the questions stations. Then they are instructed to write down on a separate sheet of paper as many responses as possible to the given question. A different student can serve as a recorder for each question. At the end of the allotted time, the groups move to the next question station and the process is repeated.

Data Synthesis Phase—In this phase, students get the chance to hear the responses of all their classmates. The teacher or an appointed student writes the various answers under each posted question, thereby leading the way to a whole class discussion of new concepts and ideas.

Final Presentation Phase—The completed posters can be placed on bulletin board, reread later for review purposes, or typed as handouts.

Cybernetic sessions are useful for all subject areas. Because they require a certain degree of movement, they appeal to middle level students' inherent need to be active.

Tutorial grouping

When students are in need of assistance, tutorial grouping is the next best alternative to direct teacher-to-student interaction. In tutorial grouping two students work together and are responsible for each other's learning. As such, the disparity between them should not be so great as to intimidate a partner. Likewise, pairs should not be so similar in terms of ability that they are unable to aid each other's progress. Learning or reading disabled, ESL, or educable mentally handicapped students are often unable to handle grade level material. Therefore, the teacher may choose to assign the majority of the class the textbook reading while tutorial groups work in topically-related alternative materials written at an easier grade level.

A management device, found useful by this author, is the lesson plan form excerpted on p.22 . This form is filled out initially by the teacher and then later taken over by the tutor and tutee as more responsibility is allotted to them. It shows how the form may be used in a science class.

Tutorial grouping is most effective when it is not used excessively. Otherwise, the chosen students may feel isolated from their classmates. When deemed necessary, the teacher may say something like, "For the first half of the period, form your tuto-

```
┌─────────────────────────────────────────────────────────────────┐
│                  Excerpt from Lesson Plan Form                    │
│                    Names:  John/Doug                              │
│                    Subject:  Science                              │
│                                                                   │
│   Date        What I plan to do today         What I did today    │
│  ─────────────────────────────────────────────────────────────   │
│   9/4      Read Gateways to Science, pages   I finished reading   │
│            24-27 with partner.  Write down   and wrote down 5     │
│            10 new ideas                      ideas.               │
│                                              Doug wrote 3 more.   │
│                                                                   │
│   9/6      Study display case on insects     I chose spiders,     │
│            in room with partner.  Choose 3   roaches, and flies.  │
│            insects.  Write 3 facts about     I wrote my facts     │
│            each from Gateways, Chapter 2.    from the book.       │
└─────────────────────────────────────────────────────────────────┘
```

rial groups and begin your next assignment. The remainder of the class will work in pairs on the textbook assignment. I will be around to assist all of you. Then, we will all see a demonstration on insect life."

Social grouping

Allowing students to work with peers of their own choosing can be most beneficial behaviorally and academically. The reward of such a grouping arrangement may be all that is needed to quiet a restless class after lunch or prior to an assembly program. The teacher need only say, "You may choose a partner with whom to work if you do so quietly." Or an alternative is to ask the class to write down the names of three preferred partners, then, as Johnson et al. (1984) have suggested, those students not selected can be grouped with others who are known to be compassionate and supportive.

Interest grouping

Capitalizing on the specific interests of adolescents is often a sure-fire way to motivate them to undertake an assignment. After the introduction of a particular unit in any subject area, the teacher can provide a list of activity or content-based choices. Some content-based choices in social studies, for example, may include collecting more information and objects related to Greece including food, climate, dress, government, etc. Some activity-based choices might involve presenting a skit, making a demonstration, engaging a speaker, developing a project, or writing a report.

References

Cuban, L. (1984). *How teachers taught: Constancy and change in American classrooms 1890-1980.* New York: Longman.

Doda, N., George, P. & McEwin, K. (1987, May). Ten current truths about effective schools. *Middle School Journal, 18,* pp.3-5.

Fader, Daniel (1976). *The new hooked on books.* New York: Berkley Publishing, .

George, P. & Lawrence, G. (1982). *Handbook for middle school teaching.* Glenview, Illinois: Scott, Foresman and Company.

Goodlad, J I. (1984). *A place called school.* New York: McGraw-Hill

Johnson, D. W., Johnson, R.T., Holubec, E.J., & Roy, P.A.(1984). *Circles of learning: Cooperation in the classroom.* Alexandria, VA: Association for Supervision and Curriculum Development.

Lipsitz, J. (Ed.).(1979). *Barriers: A new look at the needs of young adolescents.* New York: Ford Foundation.

Lounsbury, J.H. (1985, November). Do Your Own Work "As I See It" column. *Middle School Journal, 17.*

Lounsbury, J., & Johnston, H. (1985). *How fares the ninth grade?* Reston, VA: National Association of Secondary School Principals.

Nickolai-Mays, S., & Goetsch, K.(1986, November). Cooperative Learning in the Middle School. *Middle School Journal, 18* .

Ratekin, N., Simpson, M., Alvermann, D., & Dishner, E. (1985, February). Why teachers resist content reading instruction *Journal of Reading, 28,* pp. 432-37.

Thomason, Julia. (1984, August). Nurturing the nature of early adolescents—or a day at the zoo. *Middle School Journal, 15,* pp. 34.

Wood, K. D. (1987, October). Fostering cooperative learning in middle and secondary level classrooms. *Journal of Reading, 13,* pp. 10-18.

Wood, K. D. (1988, May). Guiding students through informational text. *The Reading Teacher, 41,* pp. 912-920.

Purpose Makes a Difference

Timothy was a talented youth, although as his English teacher I must confess that the mark I gave him at the end of each of the first two marking periods did not in any way reflect his inherent ability.

In the comments I penned on his report card, opinions were expressed concerning his indifference, his uncooperative attitude, and his lack of effort. When Tim's second report was returned to me, I noticed that Tim's father had written on the space reserved for parents' reactions the pithy comment, "I am dissatisfied, too."

But the situation changed markedly in February. By chance I learned that Tim was interested in tennis. I asked him to stay after school, and in the conversation I mentioned some of the major tournaments I had seen.

Because of his interest, I invited him to my home on a Saturday afternoon to meet my eldest son, who had acquired some prominence as a local net star.

When Tim left my house, after a demonstration of tennis strokes, he took with him a half-dozen books on court techniques and strategy.

Frequently thereafter he stayed after school to talk to me about his reading. He developed an eagerness to give expository talks to his classmates on his hobby. He write several papers on tennis ethics and the lessons taught by the lives of great net stars. His paper on tennis ethics he must have re-written at least a dozen times before it was accepted by the school literary magazine.

I believe no one in the class read or wrote more than he did during the next six weeks. His classmates obtained a liberal education in the romance of tennis.

When I totaled his grades for the next report card I was surprised to see the great advances he had made in his knowledge of and skill in English. When I inscribed his mark on his card I wrote, "Timothy has made rapid advances recently as a student, and I congratulate him."

Back came the father's response. "You give my son too much credit, sir. It is you who should be congratulated, for the rapid advances you have made recently as a teacher."

How to use cooperative learning strategies across the curriculum

Teachers can choose from a variety of cooperative learning arrangements which are easy to implement and appropriate for all subject areas.

The topic of cooperative learning is of such significance that it cannot be covered sufficiently in a single strategy. Provided here are additional strategies for promoting cooperative learning in middle level classrooms. Descriptions are given for each strategy along with suggestions on how these strategies may be employed in various subject areas.

Dyadic Learning—Larson and Dansereau (1986) recommend having students work in dyads (pairs) to study their subject area assignments. Each must read a segment (from a paragraph up to two pages) of their textbook or assigned selection. The other partner assumes the role of "listener/facilitator" by correcting errors, adding information, or clarifying concepts. Together they can draw charts, maps, outlines, graphs, pictures or anything that will assist in furthering their understanding and recall. After each segment of text is read and discussed, the partners switch roles. At any point in the lesson, the teacher may call for a class-wide discussion of the textbook concepts.

Group Communal Writing—The improvement of students' writing proficiency is gaining widespread attention throughout the country. Group communal writing is a means of incorporating writing practice throughout all subject areas with minimal preparation, instruction, and evaluation time.

In this approach, each heterogeneous group of four students composes only one product between them. Students are able to contribute their individual strengths to the composition process which may range from spelling to proofreading, to topical knowledge. Consequently, the process of writing is modeled for those with less experience and everyone, regardless of ability level, can make a contribution.

Group members can be assigned different roles such as content editor, researcher, proofreader, or recorder, which can be rotated periodically. After the assignment is completed, group members all sign the paper to indicate agreement. A grade is given to the group to further recognize the collaborative effort. Thus, a teacher of any subject area can offer one or more writing assignment choices and circulate around the groups to provide assistance.

Associational Dialogue—The associational dialogue is a component of a strategy called free associational assessment (Wood, 1986) which uses students' free recalls as a means of evaluation. The dialogue portion can be used separately as an aid to the oral review process.

The Mountain West States: Land and Climate

List of Concepts, Places, People
timberline
continental divide
arroyo
semidesert
rain shadow

Student Free Recalls of "Associational Clusters"
"Continental Divide"

Student A —   An imaginary line like the Prime Meridian, but it's located in the Rockies. It divides the flow of rivers. Rivers on the east side flow east. Rivers on the west side flow west. On our trip out west, people called it the Great Divide.

Student B —   The continental divide determines which way rivers will flow. The Snake River, on the west side, flows west. The Yellowstone River, on the east side, flows east. The Blue River, near us, must flow to the east because it is east of the continental divide.

The teacher begins by preparing a list of the most significant concepts in the lesson to be taught. Students are to take notes on these concepts from class demonstrations and the textbook until they have "associational clusters" of relevant information. The teacher should encourage them to use information from their own experiences to further assist in retention. An abbreviated list for a social studies lesson is shown above. Although students A and B have responded to the stimulus word, "continental divide," differently, both have sufficiently captured the essence of the concept. Note how both students have included familiar information to extend their understanding.

Next, with the original list unmarked, the students can look at each concept and then mentally or subvocally recite as much of the associated content they can recall. This recitation continues until they feel they can comfortably associate the word with the related content. The process can be done at home, in class under teacher guidance, or both.

Then, class time should be provided for students to work in pairs, engaging in the associational dialogue by discussing each concept in their own words. With concept lists in hand, the students recall from memory their individual associations, elaborating on each other's contributions with their own anecdotes. The teacher can circulate amongst the pairs to clarify important terms and provide further information.

After the student dialogue review, the teacher may choose to discuss selected concepts with the class as a whole, eliciting their contributions and filling in gaps where needed.

Generic Lesson Grouping—Described by Nelson-Herber (1988) is a method for grouping which is appropriate for a variety of purposes. Although Nelson-Herber did not name this procedure, it can be called "generic lesson grouping" because of its versatility in making any reading assignment more comprehensible to all students and because it extends across the pre-reading, reading and post-reading phases of the instructional lesson. A distinguishing characteristic of this form of grouping is the nature of the roles assigned to each group member before the lesson proceeds. Roles such as *checker* and *encourager* ensure that compassion is shown for fellow students and that no one's needs are overlooked.

To implement generic lesson grouping, begin by asking students to move into groups of five and to write down as many words they can think of on the specified topic. In a social studies class, such a topic might be "Life in Japan." This brainstorming activity serves to activate students' prior knowledge of the topic before reading, thereby establishing a firm foundation on which to base the new learning. *A recorder* for each group writes down the contributed words or phrases. Next, the groups share their contributions and the class, as a whole, discusses how each word relates to the topic. From these words, the teacher and students construct a graphic organizer or web, a visual representation which uses connecting lines to show the relationships between key concepts. (see Strategy 21 for more details on this procedure).

A web in social studies, for example, may include categories such as climate, food, people, government, and the history of Japan. After the teacher asks the students to make predictions about the selection, they can begin the reading assignment. The teacher can develop a set of 5-6 questions to accompany the reading. The questions should be answered collectively by the group members. In each group a *leader* is designated to read the questions and start the reading and searching process. During the reading, the more proficient readers can assist the less able readers with difficult words and concepts. Group members then address each question, presenting evidence from the text for their responses.

A recorder writes down the answers as a *checker* ensures that everyone understands the answers offered and where they can be found. Then, an *encourager* is designated to make sure that all group members have a chance to participate and that they are praised for their contributions. During the grouping process, the teacher circulates, answering questions and providing assistance or supervision when needed.

Finally, all of the groups merge their answers by engaging in a discussion. Students are asked to explain variations in their responses by presenting evidence from the text or their prior experiences. What results is an activity in which all ability levels, even the less able readers, can participate and benefit from the group interaction and multiple recitations of the content.

Random Grouping—In some instances, it may be necessary to group students randomly. Merely directing the students to "pair up with someone seated near you" or "get into groups of four" can make the math word problems, the grammar exercises, or the science textbook questions more understandable to more students. Another way of randomizing students is to have them count off by 2s, 3s, or 4s depending on the group size needed.

Base Grouping—Johnson and Johnson (1985) have found what they call base or home groups very useful. Students within a class are assigned to a base or a home group at the beginning of the year. Then, when deemed necessary, usually 5 to 10 minutes before the beginning of the lesson, the teacher calls the students into their base groups. Here, they have the opportunity to greet classmates, discuss the previous night's homework, confer on a project, or relate an anecdote relevant to an assignment. After trying it with graduate students, Johnson and Johnson maintain that this time begins the class on a positive note since it allots students an opportunity to informally interact with their peers on academic matters.

Needs Grouping—Sometimes it is necessary to group students according to their strengths and weaknesses in a particular area. Unless the teacher has a systematic plan for ongoing assessment, these needs can go unnoticed until the first test or even later. Two methods for determining students' needs are l) pre- and post- testing, and 2) arranging assessment tests topically.

Pretests can be developed before teaching a unit on grammar, for example, to determine students' knowledge of comma usage, end-of-sentence punctuation or rules of capitalization. Similarly, they can be used to preassess students' understanding of math concepts and computations. In this way, the teacher can eliminate the teaching of unnecessary material and find out who has specific needs. Post-tests can be used after the instructional lesson to ascertain who has or has not mastered particular skills or concepts.

By arranging chapter or unit tests topically, the teacher can evaluate what students have learned and what they still need to know. A grammar test arranged topically would have categorically grouped the items related to subjects, predicates, or verbs together. By using a grid such as the one shown here, the teacher can judge if additional explanation of concepts is needed for the entire class or for specific students. The teacher can use a simple + if the majority of items on a particular topic were mastered or a - if they were not. As the grid indicates, the students profiled could be grouped for more instruction in "causes of" and "controlling" pollution, which are their weakest areas. Another possibility is to have students who performed better on the test explain the concepts to those whose test performance suggests a lack of understanding (See Wood, 1985 for more details) . ♞

Partial Class Profile, Science Unit: Environmental Pollution							
	Topics						
Student's Name	Air	Water	Soil	Noise	Solid Water	Causes	Controlling
1. Ryan	+	+	+	+	+	-	+
2. Eric	+	+	-	-	-	+	-
3. Shannon	+	-	-	+			-
4. Tara	+	+	-	+	-		-
30.							

References

Johnson, R. T., & Johnson, D.W. (1985, July-August). Student-student interaction: Ignored but powerful. *Journal of Teacher Education. 36* , pp. 22-26.

Larson. C. O., & Dansereau, D.F. (1984, February). Cooperative learning in dyads. *Journal of Reading, 27*, pp. 458-60.

Nelson-Herber, J. (1988, June/July). Cooperative learning: Research into practice *Reading Journal, 5*, p. 16. Newark, DE: International Reading Association.

Wood, K. D. (1987, October). Fostering cooperative learning in middle and secondary level classrooms. *Journal of Reading, 13* , pp. 10-18.

Wood, K. D. (1985, November). Free associational assessment: An alternative to traditional testing. *Journal of Reading, 19* pp. 106-111.

How to promote cooperative learning through the *Interactive Reading Guide*

This reading guide encourages students to share responses and discuss their answers.

At first glance, all of the students appear to be reading their textbooks silently. Suddenly, with no teacher direction, several students begin putting their desks together and talking to one another. In another corner of the room, two students are jotting down notes to one another.

Is the teacher out of the classroom? Or has the teacher lost control of the students? On the contrary, in this instance, the teacher is employing a new strategy for promoting cooperation in the reading and learning of textbook material—the *Interactive Reading Guide* (Wood, 1988).

The interactive reading guide is similar to a typical reading or study guide in that it uses questions as an accompaniment to reading text to reduce the amount of print students must deal with at a given time. It is unlike the typical guide in that students are not sent off to work individually or merely asked to turn in their assignments when finished. Instead, the teacher-directed guide is designed to lead students through the reading of textbook material in orchestral manner, sometimes requiring responses from them as individuals, small groups, pairs, or as a class. Also, students are asked to do much more than answering the literal level, multiple choice, or fill-in-the-blank questions which are typically found at the end of textbook chapters. At various points in

their guided reading, students may be asked to predict what may occur next, develop associations, discuss a segment of information with their partner, read and retell the content in their own words, or contribute their free recalls of the material to the class.

An interactive reading guide developed for a middle school social studies chapter on "The Middle Atlantic States" is provided together with an example that shows how the guide can be adapted for a ninth grade general science lesson on "Water: A Basic Resource" (p. 30).

As can be seen, the textual material is divided into manageable units. Then, after each segment is completed by the pairs, groups, or individuals, the class as a whole may discuss the responses. Although designed for the class to proceed through the guide together, the teacher may want to make adjustments by permitting advanced students to proceed ahead or by setting a time limit on certain segments to expedite the guide's completion.

A most efficient way to develop several interactive reading guides, especially if a teacher is responsible for more than one subject area, is to use the stem of the questions as shown in the examples and then add the relevant content and page numbers. In science, for example, a question might read, "Before reading, write down everything you can think of on

INTERACTIVE READING GUIDE
Chapter 16—"The Middle Atlantic States Today"

Interaction Codes:
Individual ◯   Pairs ⬭   Group ⬬   Whole Class ◯

1. In your group, write down everything you can think of on the following topics related to the Middle Atlantic States. Be prepared to share these associations with the class.

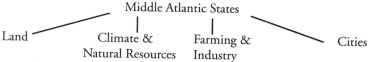

Middle Atlantic States

Land   Climate &   Farming &   Cities
         Natural Resources   Industry

2. With your partner, discuss and record some things you have learned about the Middle Atlantic region after studying the map on page 311 .

3. In your own words, define "buy" and "harbor". Locate the New York, Chesapeake and Delaware Bay areas.

4. After reading each section on pages 311-312, jot down three things you have learned about the mountains, rivers, and lakes of this region. Share this information with your group.

5. Read to remember all you can on pages 313-314 about the climate and national resources of the Middle Atlantic region. The associations of the class will be written on the board.

6. a.   Take turns "whisper reading" the four sections on "Farming and Industry" on page 315.
   After each section retell, with the aid of your partner, the information in your own words.
   b.   What have you learned about the following: poultry farms, truck farms, the manufacturing belt, petrochemical industries and still manufacturing?

7. With your partner, use your prior knowledge to predict if the following statements are true or false *before* reading the section on "Cities." Return to these statements *after* reading to see if you have changed your view. In all cases, be sure to explain your answers. You do not have to agree with your partner.
   a.   New Jersey is the most densely populated in the country.
   b.   The majority of people in the Middle Atlantic region reside in the rural areas.
   c.   Ports help commerce.
   d.   The area from Boston to Washington is one big city.

8. Read the section on "Cities." Each group member is to choose a city, show its location on the map on page 31 and report some facts about it.

9. Return to the major topics introduced in the first activity. Skim over your chapter reading guide responses with these topics in mind. Next, be ready to contribute, along with the class, anything you have learned about these topics.

the topic of pollution." Similarly. a guide for a chapter in a health might include questions such as "With your partner, jot down five things you have learned after reading the section on Components of the Eye."

An interactive reading guide could be developed to assist students in an English class comprehend a literature selection. Such a guide could be used to point out figures of speech, stylistic conventions such as foreshadowing or flashbacks, or it could stimulate students' predictive abilities by asking them to guess what a character might do next or suggest some alternative endings.

Yet another way the elements of the interactive guide can be used is to assist students in following directions. Every teacher has experienced the frustration of explaining the directions of a lesson only to have hands go up requesting that the same information be repeated or to have groups of students whispering amongst themselves because they did not hear the directions. To circumvent this problem, in

INTERACTIVE READING GUIDE

Chapter 11—"Water: A Basic Resource"

1. In your groups, write down everything you can think of related to resources. (A resource is something in nature that is valuable to mankind.) Each group will offer at least one resource to be written on the board and the whole class will discuss the various resources.

2. Read the topic "From Land to Sky" (p. 280). Close your books and answer the following questions: Where is most of the earth's water stored? How does water move from the earth to the sky? How does water move from the sky to the earth? What is this water movement called? In your groups, check and discuss your answers.

3. In your pairs, "whisper read" the three paragraphs under the section "Evaporation" (p. 280-1). With the aid of your partner, retell this information in your own words.

4. Read to remember all you can about "Downhill to the Ocean" (p. 281-2). The associations of the class will be written on the board and discussed.

5. Read "The Underground Route" (p. 282-3) and write three questions on the topic for your partner to answer.

6. Read the section "Aquifers and The Water Table" (p. 283). Answer and discuss the following questions:. a. Discuss the relationship between porous and impermeable rock in forming aquifers. b. What is occurring in an aquifer when the water table is dropping?. c. What is occurring in an aquifer when the water table is up?

    d. How do aquifers affect your life?

Contributed by David Lowe,
Knox Middle School,
Salisbury, N.C.

math class, for example, the teacher may list the day's directions on the board in the following manner:

— In your groups, try to recall everything you can remember about yesterday's lesson on fractions. Refer to the class notes and the introductory lessons on page 192 as needed.

— With your partner, read the directions on page 193. If you still have questions, ask your group members for assistance. Do the first five problems in pairs.

— Do the last five problems on page 193 individually.

During this time, the teacher is available for assistance by continually circulating among the groups or pairs as needed. Students in this hypothetical class have been taught from the beginning of the year to rely first on their peers for assistance and next on their teacher. With teacher-granted permission to request help from their peers, lesson pacing is maintained. Students who understand the assignment can proceed without being deterred by the questions of their classmates. In addition since middle level students are often reluctant to admit in front of a class that they do not understand an assignment, they are less threatened in a pair or small group situation.

It is imperative that the small groups or pairing arrangements be predetermined before a lesson begins. These arrangements can and should be flexible with changes made whenever the teacher feels it is warranted.

A Final Note

Strategy 19 lists several "Suggestions for Optimal Success" which should be adhered to when employing any type of reading or study guide. One of the most important of these suggestions is not to overdo the reading guide concept. Guides should not be developed for every chapter in a textbook. When used judiciously, the interactive reading guide can be a welcome vehicle for fostering peer cooperation and for motivating students to want to read assigned material.

Reference

Wood, K.D. (1988, May). Guiding students through information text. *The Reading Teacher, 41*, pp. 912-920.

How to effectively implement cooperative learning

Research indicates that cooperative learning can be a powerful mode of instruction when the guidelines described here are followed.

For decades, finding the best approaches for meeting the needs of individual students has been a major concern of educators. One highly touted attempt to meet student needs is programmed learning which emerged in the sixties under the influence of behaviorism. In programmed learning each student is given an assignment in a commercially prepared workbook or "machine" and allowed to work through the material at his or her own pace. Immediate knowledge of results is usually provided so students can determine if their chosen answers are correct or incorrect.

Highly prevalent in the seventies and in existence today is the mastery learning concept with its diagnostic-prescriptive approach and classroom management systems. This and similar approaches took over many subject area classrooms, especially in math, reading, and language arts. The diagnostic-prescriptive approach shares some similarities with programmed learning in that students proceed through material at their own pace. First, however, a student is given a diagnostic pretest on a specific skill. If the criterion level is not met, the student is assigned additional work in that area. A post-test is then administered and if mastery is achieved, the student exits from that task and proceeds to the next hierarchically arranged skill.

While some of the elements of these approaches for individualizing instruction have merit, many infractions of good teaching practices have resulted from their implementation. For example, in a typical classroom based on these notions of individualized instruction, students enter the room at the start of the period, pick up their assigned folder, and proceed to work through the skills exercises assigned. Students have no excuse to ask for assistance from a peer or share an idea since all are given different assignments. Consequently, no student-to-student interaction is observed and none is encouraged. Likewise, since the assignments for the class are varied, there is no room for teacher demonstrations, modeling and guided practice—components that we have come to recognize as essential to good teaching.

With the emphasis in the eighties on effective teaching and "best practices," we must reconceptualize our thinking about previous concepts of individualized instruction. We now know that little can be learned in an atmosphere that is constricted with silence and that the best approach to learning is to allow students to help other students. Indeed, in middle level schedules where teachers may be responsible for over 150 students, it is empirically unsound and humanly impossible to give everyone a different assignment. What can be done is to employ a variety of grouping strategies so that students can be responsible for helping their peers. In this way, the teacher is using the best resource available for individualizing instruction—the students themselves.

What research reveals about the benefits of cooperative learning

The earliest study on cooperative learning reported in the professional literature dates back to 1897. Since that time, hundreds of studies have been conducted attesting to the validity of employing grouping techniques in the classroom. Prominent educators such as John Dewey and Colonel Frances Parker long ago advocated classrooms in which learning must be a cooperative enterprise. More recently, Pearson and Raphael (1992) have suggested that information can be conveyed via the notion of a "cognitive apprenticeship," which is based on the model of "mentor helping novice" that has characterized entry into certain crafts and professions.

Interest in grouping has extended beyond the United States into an international effort with countries such as Israel, West Germany, Canada and Nigeria, to name a few, involved in research. According to Johnson and Johnson (Brandt, 1987), there is more evidence for cooperative learning than any other aspect of education.

Through an analysis of the voluminous research on grouping (Johnson, Maruyama, Johnson, Nelson and Skon, 1981, and Slavin, 1983), it has been consistently shown that students in cooperative learning situations score higher on achievement tests than students learning by other methods. Further, according to reviews by Lehr (1984) and Johnson and Johnson (1985), many other benefits of cooperative learning have emerged. Specifically, students consistently engaged in cooperative learning arrangements have

    a. a higher motivation to learn,
    b. greater intrinsic motivation,
    c. shown improvement for both tutor and tutee,

    d. demonstrated more positive perceptions about the intentions of others,
    e. displayed a decrease in negative competition,
    f. shown a greater acceptance of differences in their peers,
    g. more positive perceptions about the intentions of others,
    h. shown improvement in their attitude to persons of different races, and
    i. displayed greater self sufficiency and a decrease in dependence on the teacher.

Despite the magnitude of these research findings, Johnson and Johnson (1985) have estimated that group learning strategies are used only 7 to 20% of classroom time. Some of the primary assumptions offered for these low figures are that l) teachers often are afraid that chaos will result if the room is rearranged, 2) middle level teachers, in particular, were often trained on a secondary model of education which promotes the lecture approach, with its straight rows and assigned seats, and 3) teachers lack knowledge of the many grouping strategies from which to choose.

The remainder of this section will address the first assumption by listing some suggestions to be followed to help ensure successful implementation of cooperative learning strategies in any classroom.

Suggestions for successful implementation

Suggestion One: Begin the year by establishing an atmosphere of responsible learning and caring in which negative comments are not tolerated. Explain to the students that for the remainder of the year, they will be asked to help and receive help from their peers, share ideas, and encourage one another through projects and assignments.

Suggestion Two: It will be necessary to discuss and then extend with such rules existing classroom rules as "stay in your groups," "speak softly," "respect others," "avoid criticism," etc. Rules can be posted in the classroom and reinforced when needed before the start of a group assignment.

Suggestion Three: To further ensure success and avoid chaos, the teacher will want to make decisions about placement in groups before beginning the lesson. This preparedness communicates to students that the teacher is well-organized and expects the same from them.

Suggestion Four: Specify in advance the academic objectives of the lesson. Explain, demonstrate, and model any skills to be learned or strategies to be employed. Lessons run smoothly when students have a thorough understanding of the tasks involved.

Suggestion Five: Specify in advance the collaborative objectives of the lesson; that is, tell students how to interact to complete a task and determine the individual roles and responsibilities to be undertaken. For example, a research group would assign roles related to researching the topic, recording the content, revising, proofreading, and editing.

Suggestion Six: While students are engaged in group learning, continually circulate and monitor to oversee the social interactions and provide assistance.

Suggestion Seven: Be sure to use a variety of grouping strategies throughout the curriculum to avoid boredom and apathy and to allow students the opportunity to work with all class members. A sample weekly schedule for a seventh grade class using some of the advocated strategies is shown below.

Suggestion Eight: In some instances, it may be beneficial to have students 1) summarize the academic content to determine if objectives have been met, and 2) evaluate the collaborative objectives to assess the group's use of effective interpersonal skills. This process is a valuable way to make continuous improvement and ensure lasting success.

A Sample Weekly Schedule for a Seventh Grade Class

	MONDAY	TUESDAY	WEDNESDAY	THURSDAY	FRIDAY
LANGUAGE ARTS	Introduce point-of-view paragraph writing assignment—model for whole class	Students work in Buddy System Groups to compose/edit	Students are paired randomly to compose a single descriptive paragraph	Students work individually and then share compositions with original Buddy System Group for editing	Students volunteer individual efforts with Whole Class Work displayed
SOCIAL STUDIES	Teacher builds background on "India" Whole Class	Group retellings of varied, topically-related material	Students begin Interactive Reading Guide on textbook chapter	Students continue Interactive Reading Guide	Teacher and students pose topics for future Interest Groups
SCIENCE	Demonstration on "Source of Pollution" Whole Class	Students read relevant textbook section—Dyadic Learning	Whole Class discussion of textbook content	Students choose related topics—form Research Groups	Research Groups continue
MATH	Teacher models use of percentages on overhead—Whole Class	Students practice in pairs—Tutorial Grouping	Students practice Individually	Progress test given	Students grouped according to need

References

Brandt, R. (1987, November). On cooperation in schools: A conversation with David and Roger Johnson. *Educational Leadership, 45* , pp. 14-19.

Johnson, D. W., Maruyama, G., Johnson, R., Nelson, D., & Skon, L. (1981). Effects of cooperative, competitive and individualistic goal structures on achievement: A meta-analysis. *Psychological Bulletin, 89* , pp. 47-82.

Johnson, R. T., & Johnson, D.W.(1985, July-August). Student, student interaction: Ignored but powerful. *Journal of Teacher Education, 36* , pp. 22-26.

Lehr, Fran. (1984, February). Cooperative learning. *Journal of Reading, 27* , pp. 458-60.

Pearson, P. D., & Raphael, T.E. (1990). Reading comprehension as a dimension of thinking. In B. F. Jones and L. I. Idol.(Eds.), *Dimensions of thinking and cognitive instruction: Implication for reform, Vol. I,* Hillsdale, NJ: Lawrence Erlbaum Publishers, pp. 209-240.

Slavin, R. E. (1983). *Cooperative learning.* New York: Longman.

Just for Fun

You work at a newsstand, where people frequently bother you by asking for change without buying anything. One afternoon you look in your depleted drawer and get an idea. You remove one coin, give it to a passing child and wait. A few moments later, a fellow walks up and says, "Can you change a dollar?" "No, sorry." "How about a half-dollar?" You glance down again. "No, not that either." "A quarter, then?" "Sorry. Not a quarter." The fellow is clearly annoyed. "How about a dime?" "Nope." "or a nickel?" (Now he's becoming snide.) "Well, no. Not even a nickel." "But I can see you have coins in your drawer." "That's right," you say with a smile. "I have $1.19!" What coins are in your drawer?

ANSWER: If you can't change a dollar; you have no more than one half-dollar; and if you can't change a half-dollar, you have no more than one quarter and no more than four dimes. If you can't change a dime, you have no more than one nickel; and if you can't change a nickel, you have not more than four pennies.

These "no more than" coins add up to $1.24, and they *will* change a dollar, which you knew when that child walked by—and that's why you gave him a nickel, leaving $1.19.

The coins you now have left—a half-dollar, a quarter, four dimes, and four pennies—won't change a dollar or anything smaller.

How to incorporate writing with subject matter instruction

Communal writing as a strategy meets several objectives and can easily be incorporated in any area using the steps described here.

Numerous research studies conducted through the years have delivered the consistent message that our nation's children are writing infrequently, and consequently, not very proficiently (Applebee, 1984; Applebee, Langer, Mullis, & Jenkins, 1990; Calkins, 1991; Reutzel & Hollingsworth, 1988). These criticisms reveal that although students spend a great deal of their school day with pencil in hand, they are typically engaged in short answer and fill-in-the-blank exercises with little opportunity to actually compose a written passage of text.

Aware of this serious academic deficit teachers have added writing instruction to their increasing list of responsibilities. To middle level teachers, who often teach over 150 students a day, the thought of having yet another subject to teach is a formidable one. When viewed as a separate subject to teach, especially to a science teacher who may not have a language arts background, writing instruction can seem like an insurmountable burden. However, when viewed as a means of teaching subject matter, the task is far less threatening and often enjoyable for both the teacher and the students.

One way to incorporate writing with subject matter instruction is to implement communal writing in the classroom. In this strategy, small groups of students put their heads together to develop a single composition between them. Communal writing is based on the extensive research on collaborative learning which has been found to positively affect everything from self-esteem to peer and race relationships (Wood, 1987).

Implementing communal writing

Communal writing is an expedient way to help students become better writers by practicing the process of writing. Students are preassigned to groups of four or five with each group becoming a "community of writers." By establishing the writing groups in advance, the teacher can ensure a heterogeneous grouping arrangement in which students are able to assist fellow students. As with any community, students work together to contribute their individual strengths to the process which may involve spelling, content knowledge, proofreading or composing, to name a few. It is important to specify the tasks each member of the group may be expected to undertake at the onset. For example, group members may elect or be assigned to such roles as researcher (if needed), content editor, contributing author, recorder, or proofreader. These roles should be rotated periodically. Some suggested role descriptions for communal writing follow:

Contributor— All group members contribute ideas related to the topic.

Recorder— Individual records the ideas suggested (in both rough and final draft stages).

Reader— Individual reads aloud the composition for the group to assess "soundness" (in both rough and final draft stages).

Proofreader— Group members (select or all) proofread the composition for punctuation, grammar, content, spelling, etc.

Editor— Group-selected individual gives final stamp of approval to composition.

Requiring the composition of a single product from each group alleviates the "I can't get started because I don't know what to write" or blank page syndrome. It also serves to contain the unfocused writer who tends to write pages of disconnected and detailed content. Grades can be given to individual members for their cooperation in the tasks or to the group as a whole for completing the project. Although a peer editing phase is an option, the teacher may decide to engage in communal writing solely for its value as either a pre-reading or background building strategy or as a post-reading or synthesizing strategy. As such, no formal editing needs to take place. However, it is recommended that communal writing, for the most part, be viewed as a means to provide writing practice for students, in which case, the assignment of a grade would not be necessary.

Story impressions

The story impressions strategy developed by McGinley and Denner (1987) enables readers to predict a story line using sequentially presented key words or phrases derived from the selection. The reason for the ordering of the concepts is to encourage students to predict a story line as close to the actual selection as possible. After reading the key phrases, readers develop an impression or anticipatory set. Then, they construct their predicted passage and use this as a blueprint or model to be confirmed or modified as they encounter the new information in the actual story. The specific procedures for introducing story impressions in the classroom follow.

Pre-assign the students to writing groups of four or five and allow them to move their desks in a composing circle, if possible. Tell them that they will work together to predict a storyline based on some clue words they will be given.

Discuss the importance of prediction to understanding by explaining that in order to predict and make reasonable guesses, readers must bring to bear all of their prior experiences on a topic. Eliciting their own background knowledge creates richer mental images and elaborations which, in turn, helps them understand.

Explain, too, that very often it is possible to make reasonable predictions about something with a minimal amount of information. Showing a portion of a familiar object or picture and having students guess the whole is one way to demonstrate this concept. Relate this to reading by telling students that previewing the title of a chapter, pictures, boldface print, and subheadings beforehand helps readers develop a mental set for the content to be studied.

Then, introduce the key words and phrases on the board or an overhead or by giving each student or group a printed copy (illustrated). Read through the words with the students and ask them to begin developing their impressions of what the story may be about. For modeling purposes, you may want to "talk through" a short example initially with the class as a whole before breaking them into small groups.

Tell the students that they will put their heads together to construct a single storyline between them. Remind them of their roles and functions within the group.

Circulate around the groups to provide assistance wherever needed. If time is a problem, which is frequently the case in middle schools, a timer may be used to give the students a specified number of minutes to complete the task.

Have the groups read their story impressions to the class and point out how varied, and yet equally acceptable, the responses can be. Pass out the original selection and have students read and make comparisons. The group concept can be continued here with students reading portions of the story and then retelling the information with group members.

When making the comparisons with the actual selection, assure students that closeness of match with the author's story is not that important. Afterwards, or the next day, the groups or the class as a whole use the key words to retell the events of the actual selection. Mention how powerful and potent key words can be in predicting and in helping us recall what we have read.

Exchange-compare writing

While the story impressions strategy is appropriate for narrative material, exchange-compare writing (Wood, 1986) is appropriate for exposition. Again, a list of approximately 10 to 15 key vocabulary terms is presented to the students. However, unlike the story impressions strategy, the key concepts here are introduced in random order. Alphabetizing the list is one way to emphasize that students can use the words in any order. Students are grouped in fours and fives heterogeneously and asked to use the words to develop a passage, predicting the actual selection. If assistance is needed, the teacher

---

Story Impressions
Language Arts
"The Fog Horn" by Ray Bradbury

It was time to turn on the *fog light. McDunn* climbed the *tower nervously. As he ascended,* he thought about the legend that *something comes* to the *lighthouse* when the *fog horn calls* in the night.

The fog horn sounded and McDunn looked out. He saw something *swimming* toward him. What could it be? He could see *immense eyes* in a gigantic head! Was it some kind of *subterranean* monster? Just then something *roared.* Was it the monster or the wind? McDunn felt his *isolation* as he looked out over the *surface* of the water, *waiting* to see or hear something in the thick fog.

Suddenly, a large dark shape came *rushing* out of the fog and *crashed* into the rocks on the beach. It was a fishing boat. When the *rescuers* found the boat crew they were not hurt, but they acted very strange. They kept saying something about a sea monster chasing their boat. But if there ever was a monster, it was *gone* now—back to the *deep.* Would it return? McDunn was sure it would.

may want to discuss the unknown word or words in a meaningful context, eliciting elaborations from the students. Or, students may choose to look up unknown words in the dictionary and select an appropriate definition.

The groups can then read their predicted compositions to the remainder of the class, discussing the differences and similarities. Then, they, in effect, "exchange" their predicted passage for the actual passage by "making comparisons" and reacting to the selection from which the words were taken as illustrated below.

Capsule vocabulary

Unlike the previous two strategies, capsule vocabulary (Crist, 1975) is used in the post-reading phase of the instructional lesson, after the reading or studying of the content. It, too, begins with the selection of approximately 10 to 15 target vocabulary terms which are displayed and reviewed. A preferred practice would be to introduce the words in the pre-reading phase and instruct students to focus on them while reading, using the context to infer their meanings. Research has shown that the mere process of targeting new words increases the likelihood that students will learn them from the context (Elley, 1989; Jenkins, Stein, & Wysack, 1984).

In the next step, the teacher, with the aid of the class, reviews each term using it in a conversational context as much as possible. Instead of listing the words on the board and giving textbook-like definitions, the teacher uses the term informally in conversational sentences to expand the meaning (see example).

Exchange-compare Strategy

Social Studies
Governments and Economic Systems

Selected words:

capitalism	production
communism	profit
competition	resources
economics	revolution
industry	socialism

Predicted passage:

The *economics* of the United States is based on *capitalism*. Natural *resources* are used for the *production* of goods. Then these goods are sold for a *profit*. Anyone can start an *industry* or a business to sell things. Businesses are in *competition* with each other. Some countries have *communism* or socialism. In Russia there was a *revolution* to make communism the form of government.

Science

Arthropods

Step one: Present vocabulary

arthropods	millipedes
exoskeleton	carnivorous
crustaceans	arachnids
gills	prey
segments	venom
centipedes	

Step two: Review definitions

Teacher: *Animals with exoskeletons, such as crabs, do not have bones. Another name for an exoskeleton is what, class?*

Students: *Armor, or a hard, rigid covering.*

Step three: In pairs, students engage in conversational dialogue.

Student A: *I guess all arthropods have an armor called exoskeletons, don't they?*

Student B: *That's right, and jointed legs. And some, like crustaceans, breathe through gills.*

Student A: *A turtle's shell is like an exoskeleton.*

Step four: Partners work together to compose a paper on topic of arthropods.

Arthropods are invertebrate animals that have exoskeletons and jointed legs. There are more kinds of arthropods than all other animal species put together. Some types of arthropods are crustaceans, centipedes, and millipedes, arachnids, and insects.

Crabs and lobsters are crustaceans. They breath through gills and their bodies are divided into segments. Centipedes and millipedes look like worms with legs. The difference between them is the number of legs on each segment. Also, centipedes are carnivorous and use poison to kill their food.

The name for arachnids came from a Greek myth about a woman named Arachne. Their bodies are divided into two main sections and they have eight legs. Spiders and scorpions are arachnids. They both kill their prey with venom. Ticks are also arachnids. They don't have venom, but they can spread diseases.

The explanations serve as a model for the next step in which students work in pairs to engage in an associational dialogue. Here, they use the vocabulary as a springboard for a conversation with their partner, checking off the terms as they are mentioned. Using new vocabulary in this way moves them beyond the rigid memorization tasks that typify vocabulary study and into a higher level of understanding and learning.

Next is the composition stage. Students are grouped in fours and fives to use as many of the target vocabulary as possible in constructing a passage. The associational dialogue and the composition steps can be timed, approximately 10 minutes each, to expedite the process. By this time, students have had numerous encounters with the vocabulary and concepts of the selection to help solidify their understanding and improve their retention.

Summary

Communal writing is one vehicle for providing writing practice that is easily accommodated to any subject area. It is a means for merging writing with the teaching of content rather than adding writing as another subject to teach. As described here, teachers will find communal writing accomplishes many tasks; it enhances vocabulary development, provides writing practice, and serves as a means to synthesize content. Most importantly, middle level students will be able to join the "writing community" with minimal risk and maximal opportunity for learning. ♞

References

Applebee, A.N. (1984). Writing and reasoning. *Review of Educational Research, 54,* 577-596.

Applebee, A.N., Lange, J.A., Mullis, I.V.S., & Jenkins, L.B. (1990). *The writing report card, 1984-1988: Findings from the nation's report card.* Princeton NJ: National Assessment of Educational Progress.

Calkins, L.M. (1991). *Living between the lines.* Portsmouth, NH: Heinemann.

Crist, B. (1975). One capsule a week: A painless remedy for vocabulary ills. *Journal of Reading, 19,* 147-149.

Elley, W.B. (1989). Vocabulary acquisition from listening to stories. *Reading Research Quarterly, 24,* 174-187.

Jenkins, J.R., Stein, M.L., & Wysocki, K. (1984). Learning vocabulary through reading. *American Educational Research Journal, 21,* 667-87.

McGinley, W.J., & Denner, P.R. (1987). Story impressions: A pre-reading/writing activity. *The Journal of Reading, 31,* 248-253.

Reutzel, D.R., & Hollingsworth, P.M. (1988). Whole language and the practitioner. *Academic Therapy, 23,* 405-415.

Wood, K.D. (1986). How to smuggle writing into classrooms. *Middle School Journal, 17*(3), 5-6.

Wood, K.D. (1987). Fostering cooperative learning in middle and secondary level classrooms. *The Journal of Reading, 13,*10-18.

All too often we give our young people cut flowers when we should be teaching them to grow their own plants.

—John Gardner

Nothing worth learning is learned quickly, except parachuting.

—David S. Brown

How, when, and where to use oral reading in the middle school

Although often criticized, there is a place for oral reading in the middle school. Here are some suggestions for where, when, and how.

Yes! When used judiciously, oral reading can have a place in middle school classrooms; and, it can be a lively way to spark interest in almost any reading or content area selection and promote positive interaction among students. Consider the following scenarios:

Classroom A:

Students in a social studies class are seated in straight rows and assigned seats. Each student is called on to read orally from the social studies textbook beginning with the first row. By the time the fourth student begins reading the first three are gazing out the window, chatting with one another, or passing notes. The next few students are busily reading ahead trying to rehearse their upcoming lines. A subsequent discussion of the story reveals that their comprehension and recall is sketchy.

Classroom B:

In another social studies class, students are asked to get in pairs and move their desks together. At times, partners take turns whisper reading paragraphs to each other. At other times, they read silently and take turns retelling the selection in their own words, elaborating on the content whenever necessary. When

asked to engage in a group discussion after completing a few pages, all have had sufficient practice with the content and information to make the lesson successful and meaningful.

In Classroom A, the teacher is employing round-robin oral reading, the practice of calling on students in serial or random fashion to read orally. Unfortunately, this practice is still alive and prevalent today in both reading and subject area classrooms. Round-robin reading typically results in students who lose their places, correct the errors of their peers, are bored and turned off to reading and call words rather than comprehend them. Consequently, the students receive little opportunity to read and make the speech match the print.

In Classroom B, the teacher has engaged the students in a variety of techniques combining both oral and silent reading. Students may be called upon randomly to read individually, in pairs, or as a group. Paired or group retelling replaces excessive reliance on the guidebook questions. Here, the end result is students who have learned to put information in their own words and monitor their own and their partner's comprehension. Such students are engaged in reading throughout the selection and enjoy the act of reading.

The Reading Phase
of the Instruction Lesson

The dilemma of what to do during the reading phase of an instructional lesson is a universal one. The pre-reading phase of an instructional lesson consists of strategies for building background knowledge of the subsequent lesson, pre-teaching significant terms, setting purposes, and relating new information to previously learned information. The post-reading phase consists of discussing the content, synthesizing the concepts, reviewing the significant vocabulary, and extending the lesson through writing, researching projects, or some other enrichment activity. Yet, the reading phase is often characterized as simply the time during which students are asked to silently read the chapter, story, or excerpt. Middle school teachers are well aware that the directive to "read silently" is not always followed. Students may see this as an opportunity to daydream, work on other assignments, write notes, or sleep with their eyes open. The teacher does have other options from which to choose, however. These options may include (a) developing a study guide (see Strategies 18 and 19 for alternative guides), (b) engaging students in the guided reading procedure (see Strategy 21), (c) developing a reaction guide (see Strategy 23) or (d) engaging them in a variety of approaches to oral/silent reading and having students retell the content to their peers.

Research support for oral reading

Research attests to the fact that oral reading can be an effective way to help students understand the meaning of text (Pearson & Fielding, 1982; Samuels, Schermer, & Reinking, 1992). Giving students the opportunity to read orally as well as silently causes them to focus on the print itself which, in turn, leads to more fluent reading. Through fluency training, students, especially poor readers, are better able to grasp the author's message as they attend to the rhythm, pitch and tone of written language (Allington, 1983a; McCauley & McCauley, 1992; Miccinati, 1985). Much success has been demonstrated using choral reading, which is a variation of oral reading, with ESL students. Choral reading is a low anxiety activity in which all students are able to participate without failure and tension. Further, the authors report that students' individual mispronunciations are "absorbed by the overriding voices of the group" and no one is put on the spot (McCauley & McCauley, 1992, p. 528).

Alternative Approaches
for the Reading Phase

There are many variations of oral/silent reading which may be employed throughout the subject areas (Wood, Algozzine, & Avett, 1993). Teachers may elect to use any one or more strategies within a given instructional lesson. With most science, social studies, or health lessons, combining one or two oral reading methods with silent reading is probably most appropriate due to the expository style of writing and the density of concepts. However, with literature selections containing much dialogue, combining a variety of approaches to oral reading can be lively and enjoyable.

Paired or assisted reading

In this approach the teacher methodically (or randomly) pairs two or more students together for the purpose of reading aloud in unison. Because more than one individual is permitted involvement, it lessens the likelihood that other students will clamor to correct the errors of their peers. The teacher may choose to read along to assist with the fluency if deemed necessary. Students find this approach satisfying because they have a partner to rely on and they rarely have to go it alone.

Cloze procedure oral reading

Here the teacher reads from a selection while the students follow along with their copy. At designated words or phrases the teacher pauses as the students "fill in the blank" with the missing words. This approach helps students maintain their places, causing them to attend to the page and make the speech-to-print match.

Mumble reading

The phenomenon of mumble reading was observed and advocated by Cunningham (1978) when she witnessed her graduate students subvocalizing as they tried to make sense out of a strange alphabet. At selected points in a story, students may be told to mumble read (read aloud softly, but under your breath) to the end of the paragraph or page.

Whisper reading

Although mumble reading is somewhat intelligible, whisper reading means carefully pronouncing the words but in a very soft voice. Students may be told to whisper read individually, with a partner or in a group.

Choral reading

When used judiciously, in combination with other methods, choral reading can be an enjoyable and engaging method to employ. Having students read in unison at a significant point in a selection can increase suspense or express an emotional reaction intended by the author.

Imitative reading

Sometimes it is necessary to assist one or more struggling readers with their pacing and fluency. While pronouncing each and every word with precision is not necessary for comprehension, demonstrating an understanding of the prosodic cues of written language is essential. The teacher may choose to read a short section (usually dialogue) in an exaggerated tone and then call on one or more students to "repeat after me" in the same manner.

Four-way oral reading (Wood, 1983)

In this approach, a combination of several methods can be used within the reading of a single lesson. For example, in a basal story, students may be told to join their partner and whisper read the first two paragraphs. Then they may be told to mumble read as a group to the end of the page. Choral reading may be used to express an important event, followed by assisted, imitative, and back to whisper reading. In these instances, the teacher leads the group in orchestral manner, maintaining a lively and interesting pace for the lesson.

Paired reading/retelling

Students can be paired to read silently or orally (using any of the methods described here) or a combination approach. After designated segments (a page, a paragraph, etc.), they can take turns retelling the information in their own words. The partners should be told to elaborate, add any missing content, whenever necessary.

A Comparison of Approaches

The following chart depicts the comparison between round-robin reading in the right column and varied approaches in the left column. The middle column represents the reading material itself, and, although divided in paragraphs, the teacher could assign students more or less to read at a time depending on the material. For example, a literature selection may contain dialogue which may be divided according to who is doing the speaking.

When round-robin reading is used in middle level classrooms, it has been observed that each class

A Comparison of Approaches		
Varied approaches	**Text**	**Round-robin reading**
Choral	Paragraph 1	Kevin
Paired	Paragraph 2	Lauren
Whisper	Paragraph 3	Eric
Mumble	Paragraph 4	Ryan
Silent	Paragraph 5	Mandy
Whisper/paired	Paragraph 6	Jacob
Silent	Paragraph 7	Daniel

member seated in straight rows and assigned seats is called on randomly to orally read a subject area or literature selection. Since students in the back of the room are unable to hear what the students in the front are reading, they frequently lose both their places and their interest. When a struggling reader's turn comes up, other students become restless and bored, often calling out the word or words missed to hasten the lesson. The teacher, too, in an attempt to ease the struggling reader's discomfort quickly calls on another student to maintain the lesson pacing. Consequently, readers who need the most opportunity for making the speech-to-print match get to read less often than their skilled counterparts (Allington, 1983b). By using a combination of approaches where students often read with someone rather than alone and where they retell the content with their peers, participation in making that all important speech-to-print match is more than tripled!

Some Final Notes

A few important comments must be made to insure successful incorporation of oral reading with the instructional lesson:

Emphasize comprehension

Remember that the most important part of reading is comprehension—not pronouncing all the words correctly. By incorporating group or paired retelling throughout a lesson and/or by incorporating questioning requiring higher level thinking, students' understanding can be increased.

Emphasize silent reading

It is generally agreed that as the grade level and proficiency level of the students increases, the amount of oral reading engaged in should decrease. Yet, there need not be a sharp demarcation between the oral reading prevalent in the elementary school and the silent reading of the middle school and high school. Instead, similar to the notion of gradual transition which marks the middle school concept itself, the teacher can make the transition to independent silent reading a gradual one. This can be implemented by phasing in paired or small group silent reading/retelling more frequently. Also, sometimes having students read a selection silently in preparation for the lively oral reading to follow can give students additional practice and confidence.

References

Allington, R. (1983a). Fluency: The neglected reading goal. *The Reading Teacher, 36,* 556-561.

Allington, R. (1983b). The reading instruction provided readers of differing abilities. *Elementary School Journal, 83,* 548-559.

Cunningham, P.M. (1978). Mumble reading for beginning readers. *The Reading Teacher, 31*, 409-411.

McCauley, J.K., & McCauley, D.S. (1992). Using choral reading to promote language learning for ESL students. *The Reading Teacher, 45*, 526-533.

Miccinati, J.L. (1985). Using prosodic cues to teach oral reading fluency. *The Reading Teacher, 39*, 206-212.

Pearson, P.D., & Fielding, L. (1982). Research update: Listening comprehension. *Language Arts, 59*, 617-629.

Samuels, S.J., Schermer, N., & Reinking, D. (1992). Reading fluency: Techniques for making decoding automatic. In S.J. Samuels, & A.E. Farstrup (Eds.), *What research has to say about reading instruction* (2nd ed.). Newark, DE: International Reading Association.

Wood, K.D. (1983). A variation on an old theme: Four-way oral reading. *The Reading Teacher, 37*, 38-41.

Wood, K.D., Algozzine, B., & Avett, S. (1993). Promoting cooperative learning experiences for students with reading, writing and learning disabilities. *Reading and Writing Quarterly 9*, 369-376.

Flying Lessons: A Reminiscence by George Melton

Modern technology not withstanding, some things were better in the "old days." Orange crates, for example. Made of real wood, they were, and strong enough to put wheels on and ride in. Rummaging around in the refuse areas behind the local groceries would sometimes be rewarded by the discovery of one or more of those wonderful containers. The cardboard boxes, or worse, yet, mesh bags, that oranges come in today, are most often no real fun at all.

One time a neighbor and I not only put wheels on such a crate, but wings, too. With great effort we got it up on the roof of his mother's garage. We drew straws to see who would pilot it on its maiden flight. He won and survived the first, and final, flight of our noble craft.

I was to become a middle level principal before I saw a better and far safer use for the crates. It was on a classroom observation visit to Miss Stady's eighth grade math class where I saw them put to a truly innovative use.

Ranged along the far wall below the window sills, stood a line of orange crates. Standing on end, each a different, bright color. And in each, on both the middle and bottom "shelves," were quantities of paper and miscellaneous objects.

As the class entered the room, each student went to one of the crates, took something from it, went quietly to his or her desk, and began to work. I had a suspicion of what was going on, but as this was something quite new to me, when an appropriate time arrived, I asked Miss Stady to explain the process to me.

"Well," she said, "my students cover a wide range of abilities. Exclusive use of the adopted text really doesn't serve their many needs. They all started the unit with the same lesson, but as I observed and corrected their work, I was able to see where their strengths and weaknesses were. Knowing that I can direct them to one of the crates, by color. There's no "slow" crate or "fast" crate. There are "process" crates. The manipulative devices teach the same things to some that complicated formulas teach to others. Really, Mr. Melton, believe it or not, they can all learn, and learn they do! You may have noticed some pairing-off. I find that letting them work together is a help to both the better and the less-able students. A bit irregular, I know. I hope you have no objections."

Objections? Even though we had yet to hear of individualization, cooperative learning, differentiated assignments, and the like, the results were plain to see. Kids were working…happily. Self-discipline replaced external control. And I knew about the standardized test scores for her classes. Always at the top. Who could possibly object?

The state department of education, that's who! They had decreed that, henceforth, a junior high teacher must have a minimum of eighteen credit hours in the subject they taught. Miss Stady had exactly two credit hours in math! Then fate intervened. As the president of the state junior high school principals' association, I was placed next to the state superintendent at an educational conference. I told him about Miss Stady and how it was going to hurt her, and the kids, when I had to take her math classes from her. "No need for that!" he said. "On your next state report, opposite Miss Stady's name, you enter those two hours and this comment, 'Personally approved by George Wilson, State Superintendent of Public Instruction.'"

Miss Stady taught math to the day of her retirement. She was ahead of her time. Some of us are still trying to catch up. And, one doesn't need to be pushed off a garage roof to "soar" via orange crates and that, at least that once, the bureaucracy bent before ability!

How to improve students' notetaking abilities

The Collaborative Listening-Viewing Guide can improve students' ability to learn from information observed and/or heard.

*R*emember Fridays in social studies class when the teacher put on the film of the week? The lights went out and the fun started. Notes were passed around the room. Friends whispered about the plans for the weekend. Some students put their heads on their desks and actually drifted off to sleep. Then, before you knew it, the film was over, the lights went on and off to math class...

This scenario may sound all too familiar to anyone who has experienced film, filmstrip, or videotape viewing, devoid of instructional guidance. In such instances, no preparation, purpose-setting, or follow-up is provided. While much has been written about how to present printed material, little is available in the professional literature on how to present information that is listened to or viewed.

Listening has long been considered one of the communication processes together with speaking, reading, and writing; yet viewing is a relatively recent addition to many curriculum guides and language arts models. While research is unavailable regarding the extent to which viewing activities have increased in today's classrooms, it is safe to say that an increase does exist. One reason is that many children's books have been adapted for television

viewing. Another reason is that many excellent educational programs appearing on Public Broadcasting System are available for classroom use. Likewise, more and more public libraries are purchasing videotapes for educational purposes. A recent grant made possible from the MacArthur Foundation partially funds popular PBS videotapes for use in public libraries across the nation. And it is easier now than ever before to find appropriate viewing material; teachers need only consult the *Educational Film and Video Locator*, a two volume set listing videotapes, their audience level, content area, and a brief description.

While research is scant on classroom viewing time, studies have shown that nearly fifty percent of the time spent communicating is spent listening (Hyslop and Tone, 1988). Research also indicates that little time is spent on teaching students how to listen and what to attend to during listening (Burley-Allen, 1982; Hyslop and Tone, 1988; Swanson, 1986). The reason for this may be uncertainty on the part of teachers regarding how to teach listening. Swanson (1986) surveyed teacher education textbooks and found that out of 3704 pages of text only 82 pages mentioned listening.

Presently, no widely disseminated framework is available in the professional literature to help teachers assist students in learning information from what they see or hear. This deficit exists despite the fact that on a daily basis students are expected to observe and listen to experiments (for example in science class), demonstrations (of procedures to be followed in mathematics), lectures given by a guest speaker (in health class) information on field trips (perhaps to a local historical site), or videotapes (to introduce a selection in language arts).

Introduced here is a new strategy, the Collaborative Listening-Viewing Guide designed specifically for the purposes just mentioned. The Collaborative Listening-Viewing Guide is a framework for taking notes from information observed and/or heard. It can be used by teachers as an organized format to follow in presenting content. Conversely it can be used by students to receive, record, and process the new content with the aid of their peers. Such a framework is needed to avoid practices similar to the one described at the beginning of this article in which students received no preview, guidance, or follow-up for the viewed material.

The guide is based on the extensive research on collaborative learning which attests to the many benefits accrued when students are encouraged to work in pairs or small groups (Johnson and Johnson, 1985; Lehr, 1984; Brandt, 1987). It is also based on studies of notetaking that suggest that recall is enhanced when students are (a) engaged in deeper processing while taking notes (Anderson and Armbruster, 1986; Bretzing and Kulhavy, 1979); (b) allowed to encode in their preferred rather than a prescribed mode (Fisher and Harris, 1974); and (c) encouraged to review to determine information not originally recorded (Henk and Stahl, 1985; Kiewra, 1985).

Described first are the five phases or components of the Collaborative Listening-Viewing Guide. Described next is a sample lesson that illustrates how it can be applied to a middle level, content area classroom.

Guide Components
Preview/review information

The "Preview Information" section can serve two functions. One function is similar to the "preview of coming attractions" prevalent in most movie theaters in which the audience receives a brief overview of what is to follow. This may consist of either a student-directed activity, a teacher-directed activity, or a combination of the two.

A student-directed activity might be a brainstorming session in which student input is elicited on a particular topic. For example, a teacher may say, "Before we see this videotape on the Vietnam War, let's find out what you already know. I'll organize your responses on the board." An activity which involves more teacher direction and less student input might be the presentation of key concepts and vocabulary to be encountered in the subsequent lesson. A lead-in statement for this activity might be, "Since our demonstration today will be on static electricity, there are a few terms you will hear that warrant explanation. I will explain the definitions and show how they will be used in the context of our demonstration."

A second function of this phase may be to review what was already learned. Sometimes a related field trip, videotape, or demonstration will follow a particular unit, chapter, or topic as a means of solidifying and extending the lesson. Consequently, the teacher directive here might be, "We have been studying Greece. Tell me what you remember about Greek customs, old and new, before we meet our guest who is a native of Greece."

Record (individually)

In the record phase, students are asked to jot down significant concepts, phrases, or events as they are listening or viewing. Approximately one third of the left-hand side of the form is reserved for a verbatim transcription of what is heard and seen. Students should be instructed to write down important points in this column, making certain they are brief and using abbreviations when possible. Brevity is suggested so that the process of transcribing does not interfere with the process of listening. It is important, too, that the notes be recorded in sequential order to facilitate the group elaboration activity which is the next phase.

Elaborate (small groups)

In this phase, the students join together in previously established small groups to elaborate on their verbatim transcription. Here, they can "put their heads together" to recall details, extend their abbreviated notes, contribute related information, and reorganize the new content in a meaningful way. This phase should take place as soon after the initial listening/viewing lesson as possible to insure that the significant information can be recalled.

Synthesize (whole class)

After the groups have met to elaborate on the initially recorded information, the class as a whole should again be consulted to provide yet a broader view on the topic. The teacher may begin this phase by saying, "What are some significant things we have learned from today's observation." Here is the opportunity to help students make generalizations about the content learned without burdening the discussion with superfluous details. Students can record on their guides the most important concepts contributed by class members.

Extend (pairs)

The extension phase of the listening-viewing guide allows students to work in pairs to (a) compose a paragraph or two consolidating some of the information, (b) design a project related to the topic, (c) develop a semantic map of the key concepts, (d) write a play or skit, or (e) conduct further research on an aspect of interest to them.

A Sample Guide

The accompanying guide depicts an excerpt from a student/small group notetaking session during and after viewing a videotape on "Oceans." In this instance, the videotape was used to provide visual background information for a science unit on the same topic.

In the preview phase the teacher began by eliciting students' preexisting knowledge of the topic in a brainstorming format and by introducing a few interesting facts as well. The student recorded the relevant information as shown. Although not obvious here, the teacher also used a map and a globe and asked students to indicate the location of the oceans.

Next the student recorded in the left hand column some key phrases and terms while viewing the video. Afterwards, the students worked in their groups to elaborate on each other's notes to trigger new recollections and to consolidate the information. Notice how content missed in the individual notetaking activity is filled in during the elaboration activity as the groups pool their recalled information.

In the synthesis phase, the entire class was asked to brainstorm and contribute their new learning. This information was then reorganized with the aid of the teacher in another format (in this case, semantic maps).

Finally, the students were given many options from which to choose for the extension/ application phase. The partners for this guide chose to come up with a question to research and answer throughout the unit on oceans.

Excerpt from a Guide for a Videotape on "Oceans"

Class: *Science*
Student's Name: *Kevin*
Partner: *Ryan*

Topic: *Oceans*
Other Group Members: *Lauren*
                                    Eric

Preview/Review: *The world is really one big ocean. 70 percent is water—not as calm as it looks—always moving. Plants and animals (some weigh tons and some can't be seen)—can change salt water to fresh water. Ocean bottom is six miles below surface (from our school to fairgrounds). Atlantic, Pacific, Indian, Arctic, Antarctic.*

Record (Individually)	**Elaborate** (Groups)
world oceans Pacific is largest	Pacific Atlantic, and Indian in order of size make up world oceans—also Arctic and Antarctic
ocean scientists	Oceanographers are scientists who study the sea
swimming easier	Swimming is easier because salt helps us float— contains common table salt.
Blue whales	Ocean is home of largest animals that ever lived. Blue whales can be 95 feet. Smallest is only 1/25000 of an inch
three types of life: nekton, plankton (jelly fish, small drifting)	Nekton—can swim around like fish, squid, whales, seals. Barracuda can swim at 30 mph. Many fish can't live everywhere in ocean because of temp- erature and food supply. Plankton—floating, drifting plants and animals (jelly fish). Benthos—plants and animals that live on the bottom of the ocean—sponges, starfish, coral, and oysters—fixed to bot- tom and can't move.

Synthesize (Whole Class)

```
          world oceans                        3 types of life
      /    /    |    \    \                /       |       \
Pacific Atlantic Indian Arctic Antarctic  nekton plankton benthos
   |      |      |      |      |             |       |       |
largest/ trade gentle upper  lower         swim  floating bottom
deepest                                      |       |       |
   |      |      |                          fish  jellyfish coral
storms/ storms typhoons                                  (sea anemones)
volcanoes
```

Extend/Apply (Pairs)

Our study question for this unit is: How old is the ocean and how did oceans begin?

49

Summary

Introduced here is a collaborative strategy for helping students learn more from what they see and hear in classrooms. It provides teachers with an instructional framework to follow to present viewing information in much the same way that they would present printed information—with ample attention to the pre-, during, and post-viewing phases. 🐎

References

Anderson, T.H., & Armbruster, B.B. (1986). *The value of taking notes during lectures* (Tech. Rep. No. 374). Urbana: University of Illinois, Center for the Study of Reading.

Brandt, R. (1987). On cooperation in schools: A conversation with David and Roger Johnson. *Educational Leadership, 45,* 14-19.

Bretzing, B.H., & Kulhav, R.W. (1979). Notetaking and depth of processing. *Contemporary Educational Psychology, 4,* 145-53.

Burley-Allen, M. (1982). *Listening: The forgotten skill.* New York: Wiley.

Educational Film and Video Locator (3rd ed.). (1979). New York: Broker.

Fisher, J.L., & Harris, M. B. (1974). Effect of notetaking preference and type of notes taken on memory, Part 2. *Psychological Reports, 35,* 384-86.

Henk, W.A., & Stahl, N.A. (1985). *A meta-analysis of the effect of notetaking on learning from lecture.* Paper presented at the 34th Annual Meeting of the National Reading Conference.

Hyslop, N.B., & Tone, B. (1988). Listening: Are we teaching it, and if so, how? *ERIC Digest, 3,* Bloomington, IN: ERIC Clearinghouse on Reading andCommunication Skills.

Johnson, R.T., & Johnson, D.W. (1985). Student-student interaction: Ignored but powerful. *Journal of Teacher Education, 36,* 22-26.

Kiewra, K.A. (1985). Learning from a lecture: An investigation of notetaking, review and attendance at a lecture. *Human Learning, 4,* 73-77.

Lehr, F. (1984). Collaborative learning. *Journal of Reading, 27,* 458-60.

Swanson, C.H. (1986). *Teachers as listeners: An exploration.* Paper presented at the 7th Annual Convention of the International Listening Association.

The Box Game—A rainy day activity

1. Shrubbery
2. Platform used by a self-appointed orator
3. A sporting event
4. Where admission tickets are sold
5. A British holiday right after Christmas
6. A good place to be, in the theater
7. Part of the bed
8. A breed of dog
9. Part of a train
10. Men wear these
11. A reptile
12. Takes pictures
13. A baby's (or child's) toy
14. Found in the kitchen, holding what's sliced
15. Kitty uses it
16. Kids take this to school
17. Kids also take this to school
18. Talks incessantly
19. The neat young lady steps out of this
20. Jackie's hat
21. Flies in the sky without a tail
22. Type of architecture for a house
23. A toddler plays in it.
24. An old-time church social
25. Plays Brahms in the nursery
26. May be found in your skirt!

How to increase understanding of text materials through vocabulary development

The two research-based strategies described here can lead to increased vocabulary knowledge as well as increased comprehension.

There is a strong relationship between knowledge of word meanings and reading comprehension (Anderson & Freebody, 1981; Davis, 1944; 1968; Thorndike, 1974). Simply stated, the greater a student's general vocabulary knowledge, the better able the student is to understand written text. Therefore, the need to develop and expand students' word knowledge cannot be overemphasized.

Existing studies have resulted in a number of important instructional implications essential to effective vocabulary development (McKeown and Curtis, 1987). One reason offered by Nagy (1988) for the failure of traditional methods of vocabulary instruction to produce significant gains in reading comprehension relates to **depth** of word knowledge.

Typically, students engage in some variation of a definitional approach in which they look up words in a dictionary, write definitions, or find synonyms. Or, they are involved in contextual approaches in which frequently there is insufficient context provided to determine the word meaning. A more effective means is to use both the definitional and contextual approaches. Such a combination approach has been shown to result in greater understanding (Stahl and Fairbanks, 1986).

In addition, findings from research indicate that vocabulary instruction is more beneficial when students are "interactively" involved in the learning rather than engaged in rote memorization of definitions (Beck, Perfetti and McKeown, 1982; Eeds and Cockrum, 1985). The term *interactive,* as used here, relates to the current view of the comprehension process which portrays readers as dynamic participants who continually merge their existing knowledge with the new content encountered in the written material.

Another important consideration when teaching vocabulary is to ensure multiple exposures to the targeted words. Typically, significant vocabulary terms are either pre-taught prior to the reading of the selection or highlighted in some manner during the reading. However, in order for new words to be assimilated, students must have multiple opportunities to encounter and use the new words (Stahl, 1986).

Lastly, instruction should lead students to acquire new vocabulary knowledge independently (Carr and Wixson, 1986). Students need to develop strategic ways to broaden their understanding of words with a minimal amount of teacher intervention.

Two approaches which use many of the principles advocated are the **Preview in Context Strategy** (Readence, Bean and Baldwin, 1981) and **the Vocabulary Self Collection Strategy** (Haggard, 1982;

1986). Both approaches involve a combination of definition and context; they dynamically engage the students in the new learning; they provide opportunities for multiple exposures to the new terms, and they encourage independent learning.

Preview In Context Strategy

The Preview in Context Strategy (Readence, Bean, Baldwin, 1981) is an expedient and beneficial way to pre-teach significant concepts from content area material. Student involvement is high and preparation time is reduced to a minimum. Essentially, the teacher need only plan in advance which words will be the focus of instruction.

Begin by selecting some important words from a passage, chapter, or segment of text to be read. Limit the number to a maximum of 5 or 6 key words. Select words which are integral to the understanding of the selection, that is, which reflect the main concepts to be studied. Next, direct the students' attention to each word as it is used in the context of the selection. This involves a simple directive such as "Open your books to the top of page 122, first paragraph and look for the sentence in which the word 'eradicate' appears." Read the sentence or sentences (if necessary to understand the meaning) aloud to the students as they follow along in their text. Then, have them read the same sentences silently.

The next step involves a teacher-directed questioning strategy to help students use the context to derive the meaning. (See the examples that follow). Lastly,

after students seem to understand the word as it is used in their textbooks, help them to relate the word to other words. Discussing similarities and differences in word parts, eliciting antonyms or synonyms or even other contexts in which the word could be used are a few of the ways a teacher can expand students' knowledge of word meanings.

Vocabulary Self-Collection Strategy

Another method of teaching and practicing the use of context to determine word meanings is the "Vocabulary Self-Collection Strategy" or VSS (Haggard, 1982; 1986). The steps which have been modified and expanded somewhat from the original version follow.

Preview in Context Strategy
Subject: Language Arts
Topic: Poetry

Text: "Preparation" (1st verse) Robert Francis

Last fall I saw the farmer follow the plow that dug the long dark furrows
Between the hillslope and the hollow...

Step One   —Select significant vocabulary. ex: "furrows"
Step Two   —Read word aloud in context.
Step Three —Have students read silently
Step Four   —Specify word meaning through questioning
            T: What does the sentence tell you about the word *furrows*
            S: They must be dug in dirt
            S: Are they the rows?
            T: You're on the right track. How were the furrows made?
            S: With the plow
            T: Then what would furrows be?
            S: Grooves in the dirt, made by a plow.
Step Five   —Expand word meanings
            T: Can you think of another way the word *furrow* might be used?
            S: Like *wrinkle*? Someone has a "furrowed brow."
            T: What facial expression might that indicate?
            S: A frown
            T: How does that relate to the meaning of *furrow* we just discussed?
            S: Well, when you frown, your face gets grooves in it.

Before beginning a lesson, or even afterwards as a follow-up, tell the students to seek out one or more new and interesting words topically related to the unit of study. The words should be chosen from an environment outside of school, if possible. Newspapers, magazines, pamphlets, television shows, newscasts, lectures, demonstrations, or trips are some of the many sources for new words.

Students can begin to keep a personal notebook or vocabulary journal using a form such as the one presented on this page. This form, while not a part of the VSS strategy, has been used successfully by this author while a teacher in the middle school. Several blank forms can be typed and mimeographed on each page for the collection of multiple entries. The journal form shown contains a place to identify for which subject area and topic the word was selected. This is particularly useful for later use and study. It is suggested that students maintain a personal vocabulary collection for each subject area. Next, the students must give the context (either oral or written) in which the word appeared. From there, they can try to deduce the meaning from the context, if possible. The "Preview in Context Strategy" presented earlier is a helpful way to provide whole class modeling and instruction in the use of context clues.

Next, the students are to select the dictionary definition which is most appropriate to the way the word is presented. Such a task should be modeled thoroughly first as students tend to write down either the first or shortest definition given. To further expand their word knowledge, a line is provided in case the new word should conjure up familiar associations, either structurally or semantically. For example, the self-selected word "pentacle" encountered in a newspaper article may remind students of the word "pentameter" in Language Arts, or "pentagon" in math or social studies. It is on this line that similarities and differences in word parts and/or meanings can be mentioned. Lastly, to enhance retention the students are to use the word in a sentence of their own construction.

When using this strategy in the classroom, students are told to write their words on the board at the start of class. In large classes, it is recommended that half the class provide the words one week and the other half the next (Haggard, 1982). Each stu-

---

Preview in Context Strategy
Subject: Social Studies
Topic: Colonial Times

Text	Citizens of all the colonies were angry about the Stamp Act. In fact, a great deal of colonial *protest* had already occurred before the trouble began in Wilmington.
Step One	—Select significant vocabulary. ex: "protest"
Step Two	—Read word aloud in context.
Step Three	—Have students read silently.
Step Four	—Specify word meaning through questioning

    T: What does the sentence tell you about the word *protest*?
    S: It has something to do with trouble.
    T: What was the trouble about?
    S: The Stamp Act?
    T: How the colonists feel about the Stamp Act?
    S: They were angry because they were against it.
    T: What do you think *protest* means?
    S: Letting someone know you're against something

Step Five —Expand word meanings
    T: Are there words we could substitute for *protest* in the sentence without changing the meaning?
    S: Dissension, rejection, revolution
    T: Do you know of other times in our history when a goverment action has met with protest?
    S: The Vietnam War, the racial problem of the sixties, nuclear waste disposal

dent is to identify the word, its definition, where it was found, and why she/he feels it is important for class study.

After the designated number of presentations, the class narrows down the list to the most essential words. The originator of the word again defines it (with teacher assistance) and the students record the words and definitions in the "Class Words" section of their notebook. For each subject area, students can have a personal collection and a class collection of the new topically/related words. The reduced list plus any others selected by the teacher can be reviewed at the end of the week and/or unit of study. In addition, other assignments can be made using the new words such as writing skills, stories, paragraphs; making puzzles; or researching the etymology (Haggard, 1982).

Summary

As can be seen, the "Preview in Context Strategy" is more teacher directed in that the teacher leads the students to understanding through extensive questioning. The "Vocabulary Self-Collection Strategy," while monitored by the teacher, is largely accomplished through the individual efforts of each student. When used together in a lesson, both approaches have the potential to maximize the acquisition of pre-selected and self-selected vocabulary—integral ingredients for improving comprehension and learning.

References

Anderson, R. C., & Freebody, P. (1981). Vocabulary knowledge In J. T. Guthrie (Ed.), *Comprehension and teaching research reviews* (pp. 77-117). Newark, DE: International Reading Association, 1981.

Beck, I. L., Perfetti, C.A., & McKeown, M.G.(1982). Effects of long-term vocabulary instruction of lexical access and reading comprehension. *Journal of Educational Psychology, 74*, No. 4 , pp. 506-21.

Carr, E., & Wixson, K. (1986, April). Guidelines for evaluating vocabulary instruction. *Journal of Reading, 29*, pp. 588-595.

Davis, F. (1944). Fundamental factors of comprehension in reading, *Psychometrika, 9* , pp. 185-97.

Davis, F. (1968). Research in comprehension in reading. *Reading Research Quarterly, 3* (4), pp. 499-545.

Eeds, M., & Cockrurn, W. (1985, March). Teaching word meanings by expanding schemata vs. dictionary work vs. reading in context. *Journal of Reading, 28*, pp. 492-97.

Haggard, M. (1982, December). The vocabulary self-collection strategy: An active approach to word learning. *Journal of Reading, 27*, pp. 203-207.

Haggard, M. (1982, December). The vocabulary self-collection strategy: An active approach to word learning. *Journal of Reading, 27*, pp. 203-207.

Haggard, M. (1986, April). The vocabulary self-collection strategy: Using student interest and world knowledge to enhance vocabulary growth. *Journal of Reading. 29*, pp. 634-642.

McKeown, M. C., & Curtis, M.E. (1987). *The nature of vocabulary acquisition.* Hillsdale N. J.: Lawrence Erlbaum Associates

Nagy, W. E. (1988). *Teaching vocabulary to improve comprehension.* Urbana Champaign: University of Illinois (NCTE/IRA). ERIC Clearinghouse on Reading and Communication Skills.

Readence, J. B. & Baldwin, R.S. (1981). *Content area reading: An integrated approach.* Dubuque, Iowa: Kendall/Hunt Publishing Co.

Stahl. S. (1986). Three principles of effective vocabulary instruction. *Journal of Reading, 29,* pp. 662-68.

Stahl, S. & Fairbanks, M. (1986). The effects of vocabulary instruction: A model-based metaanalysis. *Review of Educational Research, 56,* pp. 72-110.

Thorndike, R. L. (1974). Reading as reasoning. *Reading Research Quarterly, 9*, pp. 135-47.

How students' experiences can be used to increase vocabulary knowledge

Here is a strategy for activating prior knowledge, enriching reading, and improving comprehension appropriate for any subject area.

One of the most important elements of an instructional lesson is what goes on before students are assigned the reading of a selection. Termed the pre-reading stage, this portion of a lesson is when the purposes for reading are set, background knowledge is elicited, and significant concepts are introduced. It is during this stage that students (especially early adolescents) either become turned on or turned off to the subsequent lesson. Consequently, what goes on here needs to arouse the interest of middle level students at the onset.

There are few better ways to motivate students than to get them to talk about their own experiences. Asking them to relate what they already know about a topic, or think they know, provides a vehicle for eliciting at least some contribution from all the class members. Merely informing the class that this week's lesson will be on Canada, or gravity, or the War of 1812 sets in motion the visual and verbal imagery necessary for a stimulating class-wide exchange of ideas and experiences.

The notion that we all possess a unique combination of experiences which can be used to aid in understanding is a prevalent one in the professional literature (Rumelhart, 1980; Spiro, 1977). "Schemata," is the name given to represent those abstract knowledge structures or "units" through which information or experiences are stored in our minds. Schema theory, then, is a theory about how knowledge is represented in memory.

A schema-theoretic view of comprehension suggests that by stimulating readers' prior knowledge (e.g. getting them to talk about their experiences), their understanding of new information can be improved and their retention increased. Ample research is available which supports this schema-theoretic view. Some of the research shows that manipulating the reader's purpose or perspective can alter how a passage is interpreted (Anderson and Pichert, 1978; Anderson, Pichert and Shirey, 1983). Other research demonstrates improved understanding when experiences are activated prior to reading a passage (Thames and Readence, 1988) or when they are enriched and elaborated after the reading (Bean, Inabinette and Ryan, 1983).

One method for accomplishing the goal of using students' experiences before, during, and after the reading of an assignment is Ogle's (1987) K-W-L Plus strategy. It consists of four phases and promotes total class involvement.

K—What I know

In the first part of this phase, the teacher asks the students to *brainstorm,* that is, contribute anything that comes to their minds about a particular topic. The information can be written on the board, a transparency, or individual worksheets in the format shown in the K-W-L-Strategy Sheet. The primary goal here is to present a topic on which the students have at least some general knowledge. Obviously this approach would not be appropriate as a vehicle for introducing entirely new concepts.

To strengthen students' thinking abilities during the brainstorming activities, Ogle suggests that the teacher ask them to support selected answers by indicating where they learned the information or by explaining how they can substantiate their responses. Such probing helps students think about the sources for their contributions and deepens their understanding of the processes by which associations are made.

The second part of the "What I Know" phase involves *categorizing* the contributed information. This step gives structure to the class-generated associations and helps students think in categorical terms. To accustom students to this part of the activity, the teacher will want to model the process by initially thinking aloud some examples.

For example, in an Earth Science unit on volcanoes the teacher might say, "I see several places where volcanoes can be found." Then the teacher can write a category such as "Locations of Volcanoes" on the board. A follow-up question could be, "What other categories can be found from the words we have listed?"

This brainstorming activity serves a diagnostic function as well. If students are unable to generate many associations, even after probing, the teacher is immediately alerted that their background of experiences is insufficient to support a conceptual understanding of the topic. Consequently, the teacher can decide to proceed no further in the lesson and instead can build their knowledge base through visual displays, demonstrations, and explanations.

Although described here as a group activity, the brainstorming phase can be conducted in small groups. A strategy sheet can be duplicated and given to each student for this purpose. Students can be assigned to small groups of four or five to develop their associations. Then a group spokesperson can offer their contributions for the entire class. Such an arrangement further reduces the risk of openly offering a response in front of the class, a fear frequently experienced by early adolescents who are known for their social self-consciousness. In addition, it reduces the likelihood that contributions will be made by a handful of the more vocal class members.

W—What do I want to know?

Since questions naturally arise from the recorded associations, these questions can form the basis for the next phase. Essentially, this is the purpose-setting phase wherein purposes for reading are determined by the students themselves. The student must determine what questions might be answered in the selection to be read. After brainstorming on the topic of volcanoes, some questions might emerge such as, "How are volcanoes formed?" "How hot is lava?" "Are there any active volcanoes in the United States?"

While it is intended that most of "phase W" be conducted as a group activity, students can also make an individual contribution by writing their personal questions on the strategy worksheets (see sample on page 57).

This phase prepares the way for the reading stage of the instructional lesson. The teacher may find it more manageable to break a chapter or selection into topically-related sections, allowing time for reflection and self-monitoring. Students need to learn that they may read only a few paragraphs before a purpose-setting question is answered. In this way, they begin to see that ways to increase comprehension involve asking and answering questions, monitoring their understanding, and actively thinking about what they are reading.

L—What I learned

While they are reading, students can be instructed to jot down, on the "L" portion of their worksheet (See Sample K-W-L Plus Lesson for Science, p. 58), any significant concepts encountered which may or may not have relevance to the questions originally posed. Then, after the reading, the

---

K-W-L Strategy Sheet
From Ogle (1986)

Name _____ Subject _____

Date _____

1. K - What We Know   W - What We Want To Learn   L - What We Learned and Still Need To Learn

2. Categories of Information We Expect To Use:

   A.   E.
   B.   F.
   C.   G.
   D.   H.

---

class can determine if the questions raised in the previous phase were adequately answered by the selection. Here they can be asked to further elaborate on a question-response by adding newly learned information.

Background knowledge displayed in the opening phase is used to understand and clarify the new concepts. For example, the teacher might say, "The word *magma* was contributed in the first part of our lesson; what have you learned about that word now?" If questions were not addressed by the selection, the students may be asked to seek further information from other sources.

The writing phase

Ogle (1987) revised the K-W-L strategy recently by adding a "Plus" to the abbreviations to symbolize a writing component. Specifically, the writing phase involves the use of semantic mapping (See Strategy 13 for a detailed description of this procedure) and summary writing. A map is a graphic representation of information which depicts the major and subordinate concepts in an organized manner.

Students can use the K-W-L worksheet to produce maps by categorizing the information listed in the "L" phase of the strategy. By asking themselves what each statement describes, they can assign the content to broader groups (see page 58). Then, with the article or topic title as the midpoint, the map can branch out to include the newly developed categories. The lines show how the major topic is related to the supporting details.

The completed maps can be done individually, in small groups, or as an entire class. To ensure a thorough understanding, it is wise to demonstrate and model the map construction process as a class before assigning independent practice. Because categorization is a higher order thinking skill, these maps help further students' understanding of the newly learned concepts.

Another alternative for the writing phase is **summarization.** The students can use their constructed maps to write logical, comprehensible sentences.

The outline for the writing activity has already been done via the map so that the students need only decide on an order and put the information in complete sentences. For the example shown the student group (working in fours) decided to write about Location, Eating Habits and Physical Traits.

Sample K-W-L Plus Lesson For Science
Topic: Crocodiles

K (Know)	W (Want To Know)	L (Learned)
many large teeth	Where do they live?	P - lay eggs
big, powerful tails	What do they eat?	L - lives in Florida
reptiles	How are they different from alligators?	E - eat birds, mammals, fish
		P - can grow to 20' in length
live in swamps	How large do they get?	P - can stay under water 2 1/2 hrs. without air
long, low body	Characteristics?	P - can outrun man
Crocodile Dundee		T - American-lives in Florida
		T - Nile - in Africa
		T - Salt Water - In India, Australia
		P - can wrestle a buffalo
		P - sometimes attacks and devours people
		L - prefers swamps, marshes, shallow water

Sample Semantic Map For Science

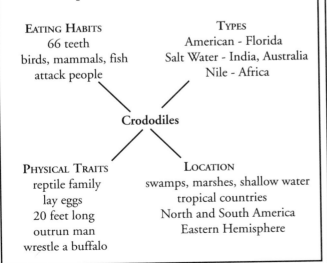

EATING HABITS
66 teeth
birds, mammals, fish
attack people

TYPES
American - Florida
Salt Water - India, Australia
Nile - Africa

Crododiles

PHYSICAL TRAITS
reptile family
lay eggs
20 feet long
outrun man
wrestle a buffalo

LOCATION
swamps, marshes, shallow water
tropical countries
North and South America
Eastern Hemisphere

Sample Summary For Science

Crocodiles are located in tropical countries. They perfer shallow, still water and can be found in marshes and in swamp lands. While North and South America have crocodiles, most of them live in the Eastern hemisphere.

Like most reptiles, crocodiles lay eggs. They can grow to a length of 20 feet and can outrun a man while on land or wrestle and devour animals as large as a buffalo. Since crocodiles can stay under water for up to $2 \frac{1}{2}$ hours without coming up for air, it is not a good idea to go swimming in swampy water.

A Final Note

Probably the most important phase of all is ensuring that the comprehension strategies learned through this activity are transferred to other reading and learning situations. After much practice under the direction of the teacher, students should be encouraged to use the K-W-L Plus strategy with its brainstorming, purpose-setting, reflecting and reorganizing phases on their own in alternative contexts. In this way, they can become the independent learners we hope them to be. ♞

References

Bean, T. W., Inabinette, N. B. & Ryan, R. (1983). The effect of a categorization strategy on secondary students' retention of literary vocabulary. *Reading Psychology, 4*, pp. 247-252.

Carr, E. and Ogle, D. (1987, April). K-W-L plus: A strategy for comprehension and summarization. *Journal of Reading, 30*, pp. 626-631.

Ogle, D.M. (1986, February). K-W-L: A teaching model that develops active reading of expository text. *The Reading Teacher, 39* , pp. 564-570.

Rumelhart. D.E. (1980). Schemata: The building blocks of cognition. In R.J. Spiro, B. C. Bruce, & W. F. Brewer (Eds.), *Issues in reading comprehension.* Hillsdale, N.J.: Erlbaum.

Spiro, R.J. (1977). Remembering information from text: The 'State of Schema' approach. In R.C. Anderson, R.J. Spiro, & W E. Montague (Eds.), *Schooling and the acquisition of knowledge.* Hillsdale, NJ.: Erlbaum, 1977.

Thames, D.G. & Readence, J.E.(1988, Winter). Effects of differential vocabulary instruction and lesson frameworks on the reading comprehension of primary children. *Reading Research and Instruction, 27*, pp. 1-12.

We learn what we live and we learn it to the degree that we live it.
—William Heard Kilpatrick

Education does not mean teaching people to know what they do not know.
It means teaching them to behave as they do not behave…
It is not teaching the youth of England the shapes of letters and the tricks of numbers; and then leaving them to turn their arithmetic to roguery and their literature to lust. It is, on the contrary, training them into the perfect exercise and kingly continence of their bodies and souls.

—John Ruskin

How to use guided imagery to enhance learning

When students are asked to imagine a scene in their heads before, during, and after reading, their comprehension and recall is enhanced.

Think of the many times we spontaneously use mental imagery when engaged in every day activities. We mentally imagine ourselves driving that new car home before we ever buy it. We think of the upcoming beach vacation and mentally take a break from our daily routine by "smelling" the salty air, "feeling" the sand, "hearing" the ocean. Or we problem-solve trying to decide what we need to take on the next business trip.

Forming mental images and verbalizing mental processes are the mind's way of symbolically representing meaning (Paivio, 1971). Imagery is a dynamic and flexible process which allows newly associated information to be stored and later retrieved. It can be a particularly useful tool to employ for problem-solving purposes especially when novel information is encountered in reading or learning situations (Kaufmann, 1979).

Numerous studies have indicated that asking students to form mental images while reading has a positive affect on learning and recall (Gambrell and Bales, 1986; Peters and Levin, 1986: Pressley, 1977). Apparently, the tendency to engage in this process is differentiated across ability levels since below average readers tend to use imagery less often than their above average counterparts when reading both familiar and unfamiliar text material (Finch, 1982).

In one study (Gambrell and Koskinen, 1982), the researchers found more support for helping students form mental images before the reading of a selection rather than after. More recently, Gambrell and Bales (1986) randomly assigned 62 fourth grade and 62 fifth grade below-average pupils to two groups: those who received imagery instructions and those who received general instructions. The subjects were asked to read two passages containing either an implicit or an explicit inconsistency. The results indicated that those subjects who were instructed to "make pictures in their minds" while reading detected inconsistencies in the text more frequently than the control group. The authors concluded that training and prompting below-average students to read using visual imaging helps them to monitor their own comprehension more effectively. Without prompting, the students tended to simply read and reread the selection when it appeared to be illogical.

Implementation in the classroom

McNeil (1987) describes a technique called "mind's eye" developed by the Escondido School District (1979). Officials from this California school system report that their yearly comprehension gains have tripled since employing this procedure. A combination of the "mind's eye" strategy and a strategy for imaging developed by Mundell (1985) results in the following suggested procedures.

FIRST—Help the students develop their visualization skills by having them create visual images of familiar objects. Simple concrete objects such as a rose, a pier, or a frog may be most beneficial for this early modeling phase. Tell the students to close their eyes and form a picture from these words by trying to sense how the object looks, sounds. feels and smells. Discuss more of the varied images with the class, being certain to reinforce the individualization of their responses.

SECOND—Proceed from individual key words to complete sentences by following the same procedures. For example, have students develop images for sentences such as: "A grandmother is cooking a turkey in the kitchen." Before eliciting their responses, have students underline the words in the sentence which were needed to help them form a mental picture. (The likely choices in this sentence are grandmother, turkey, and kitchen). Students can be asked to describe their own or a relative's kitchen and elaborate on what else and why she may be preparing this meal.

From these personally relevant examples, the teacher can move to sentences which are more content specific. These sentences can be drawn from material to be read in class.

"An amoeba will move slowly across a slide." (Science)

"Custer told his men to stop on the hill before they reached the campsite." (History)

Again, have the students underline or at least select the words with the most "picture potency" and then close their eyes to form their images. Probing questions can be asked such as: "What do you see in your mind?" "Are there any prevalent smells?" "What do you feel—emotionally or tactilely?"

THIRD—Before reading have students turn to a short selection or excerpt in their textbook or other classroom reading material. Tell them they are going to make "pictures" or a "movie" as they read through the passage. Instruct the class to select the key words in the title and try to describe everything that comes to their minds. Discuss the contributions made by the class.

FOURTH—During reading assign the students to pairs and tell them to underline lightly in pencil or put a check over the key words in the first topically relevant section often signalled by subheadings. After each dyad has discussed their images with their partners, elicit some responses from the class. The teacher should proceed in this manner for a few more sections until the class seems to have a comfortable grasp on the concept of applying this process to longer discourse. They can continue working in pairs, discussing their images, using probing questions, and even making graphic representations of the information if necessary.

FIFTH—After reading follow up with a class-wide discussion of the content, asking for elaborations and inferred details whenever appropriate. Another option to further extend the lesson is to engage the students in a writing activity or to give them an objective or subjective test.

Application across the subject areas

Guided imagery is an appropriate strategy to use in any subject area. The first illustration (page 62) shows its applicability to a typical literary selection. Notice how the "imaging" has caused students to make some predictions regarding possible story outcomes. The social studies lesson excerpt (page 63) illustrates the vast elaborations and inferences generated from visual imagery. The responses in the science lesson (page 64) capture the students' vicarious fear of a pending "tsunami."

Excerpt from a Guided Imagery Lesson
Subject: Literature "Lost Chance"

The old man was feeble. He could barely walk across the room to answer the door. His mouth dropped open when he saw his sister after all these years.

Teacher Probing Questions	Student Responses
1. Describe the old man and his environment—his dress, his surroundings.	**Student A**—He has strands of gray hair on his head. His mouth quivers as he talks and his hands shake.
	Student B—He is wearing a plaid, flannel shirt and wrinkled tan pants.
	Student C—He uses a cane to walk and sits in the same chair everyday.
2. How do you envision his sister?	**Student D**—She is much younger although still an older woman.
	Student E—I think she's after whatever money he has.
	Student F—I think she's sincere. She's been searching for him for a long time and wants a family reunion.

Excerpt from a Guided Imagery Lesson
Subject: Social Studies "California Gold Fever"

In 1849 many people moved to California any way they could. Word spread throughout the world that gold was found at John Sutter's mill. Many people made their money selling mining supplies to the newcomers.

Teacher Probing Questions	Student Responses
1 . What comes to your mind after reading the title?	**Student A**—I see people everywhere arguing, dealing, digging.
	Student B—I see a wagon train of people and wooden cars filled with shovels.
2. Tell how people got to Sutter's Mill	**Student C**—Some rode on horseback.
	Student D—Boats, wagons
	Student E—On foot, in carriages.
3 How were they dressed?	**Student F**—The woman wore bonnets and long dresses; the men wore boots, chaps and heavy shirts.
	Student G—Yes. and their clothes were dirty and dusty because they could not get cleaned regularly.
4. Describe the scene you see when mining supplies are being sold.	**Student H**—I see a store with a wooden floor and shelves filled with picks, shovels, and tin pans.
	Student I—I see men arguing over the high prices.
	Student J—Yes. One, the miner, has a beard and appears tired but eager, the other one, the storekeeper, wears an off-white shirt with a black band on his upper arm.

Excerpt from a Guided Imagery Lesson
Subject: Science "Earthquakes"

In addition to the violent movements of the earth's surface, earthquakes can cause huge sea waves that devastate the land. These waves, called by their Japanese name "tsunami," often occur in the Pacific Ocean where there is a greater prevalence of earthquakes.

Teacher Probing Questions	Student Responses
1. Describe what you see happening around you as an earthquake begins to occur.	1. Student A—The Weaver Building in the center of town begins to quiver and is the first to fall. Student B—People are running, screaming, covering their children. Student C—An alarm sounds and everyone heads for the basement of the school.
2. Your home near the ocean is threatened by a "tsunami." Tell what you see.	2. Student D—A huge, overpowering, dark blue and white wave is above me. I scream and run. Student E—The land is drowning in water. People drift by in floats or on pieces of wood. Student F—The entire atmosphere is darker. Whole houses are under water. People try desperately to get to dry land—running, swimming, clinging to their belongings.

Summary

As can be seen from the examples shown, visual imagery is an excellent tool for broadening students' conceptual understanding of subject area material. It is easy to implement, appropriate in numerous circumstances, and motivating to even the most reluctant adolescent ♞

References

Escondido School District (1979). *Mind's eye.* Escondido. CA: Board of Education.

Finch, C. M. (1982). Fifth-grade below average and above average readers' use of mental imagery in reading familiar and unfamiliar text. Paper presented at the National Reading Conference. Clearwater Beach, Florida (ERIC Document Reproduction Service No. LD228-634).

Gambrell, L. B. & Bales, R.J. (1986, Fall). Mental imagery and the comprehension-monitory performance of fourth and fifth grade poor readers. *Reading Research Quarterly, 21* (4), pp. 454-464.

Gambrell, L. B. & Koskinen, P.S. (1982, March). Mental imagery and the reading comprehension of below average readers. Situational variables and sex differences. Paper presented at the annual meeting of the American Educational Research Association. New York.

Kaufmann. G. (1979). *Visual imagery and its relation to problem solving.* New York. Columbia University Press.

McNeil, John D. (1987). *Reading comprehension: New directions for classroom practice.* (Second Edition) Glenview. IL: Scott. Foresman and Company .

Mundell. Dee Dee (1985). *Mental imagery: Do you see what I say?* Oklahoma City. OK: Oklahoma State Department of Education.

Paivio. A. (1971). *Imagery and verbal processes.* New York: Holt. Rinehart and Winston.

Peters, E. E. and Levin, J. R. (1986). Effects of a mnemonic imagery strategy on good and poor readers' prose recall. *Reading Research Quarterly, 21,* 161-178.

Pressley, G. M. (1977). Mental imagery helps eight year olds remember what they read. *Journal of Educational Psychology, 68,* 355-359.

How to teach vocabulary in the subject areas

Semantic mapping uses students' background knowledge to aid in learning new vocabulary.

Think back to Teacher X whose primary approach to teaching science vocabulary was to list thirty words on the board and have the class "look them up" in the dictionary. Recall, too, how you and your partner divided the list in half and proceeded to write down the first, or the shortest, definition available. Whether it fit the context in which the word would appear was unimportant. Like most middle level age students, the main concern was to get the assignment finished.

Unfortunately, Teacher X was probably taught using a similar method—more evidence that poor teaching methods tend to perpetuate themselves. Such methods do little to give students a conceptual understanding of subject matter vocabulary.

Any good teacher is aware that students who know the vocabulary of a course tend to understand the content of the subject matter as well. In fact, as early as 1944, Davis found that word knowledge is the most potent contributor to overall comprehension. More recent research also supports this finding (Hayes and Tierney, 1982).

Along with word knowledge, prior knowledge and experiences in general have also been proven essential to the comprehension process (Spiro, 1977; Rumelhart and Ortony, 1977). In essence, vocabulary is a means for labeling these experiences stored in our minds. According to Johnston and Pearson (1982), prior knowledge, including an understanding of the significant vocabulary in a lesson, is the best predictor of comprehension—more powerful than measures of reading ability or achievement.

Described here is a strategy called semantic mapping (Johnson and Pearson, 1984) which uses students' background in the learning and retention of new vocabulary. Semantic mapping has appeared under various names in the literature, for example, semantic webbing (Freedman and Reynolds, 1980) and fact analyzer or FAN (Swaby, 1984), to name two. Regardless of the label enjoyed, it is essentially a diagrammatic representation of the key concepts in a unit of instruction.

Semantic mapping can be used throughout the three major phases of the instructional lesson: pre-reading, reading and post-reading. The pre-reading phase of an instructional lesson may well be the most important phase of all for it is here that students' interest in the material is either captured or lost. Also, in this phase, background information for the selection is presented, key concepts are introduced, prior knowledge is elicited and assessed, purposes for reading are determined.

In the reading phase, purposes are followed as readers merge their preexisting knowledge with the new knowledge presented in the text. The post-reading, or follow up, phase is the vehicle for thoroughly synthesizing the new with the known. Here, key terms are reviewed, major concepts are discussed and summarized, and additional questions are raised. Further, the lesson may be extended to include writing, illustrating, developing or researching relevant topics.

Pre-reading phase

Begin by asking students to contribute all they can about the given topic. This can be accomplished by focusing their associations through the use of question probes. For example, on the topic of "volcanoes," the teacher may write categories on the board such as "Characteristics," "Effects," "Places Most Often Found," or "Names."

Map categories, as supplied by the teacher, can often be derived from the headings given in the textbook selection to be read. These categories can be highlighted with a circle. Then students can volunteer information from their background knowledge for each category shown, contributions are subsequently written on the board in relation to the major categories.

Another very thorough, but more time consuming alternative is to list all of the student contributions on the board in any order given. Then the students can be asked to group these concepts based on their common elements. The students themselves come up with the categories or labels for the terms given. These labels and their corresponding terms

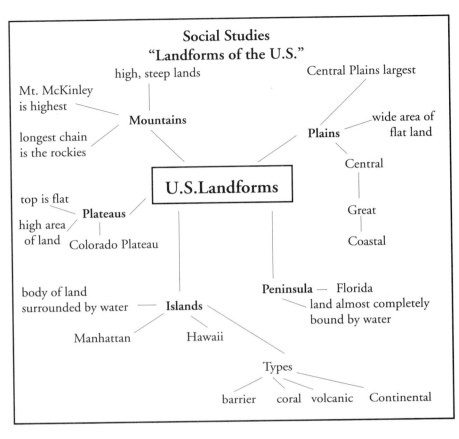

can be arranged in a "map" or "web" like manner as decided by both teacher and the class.

In either of the two alternative methods shown, the teacher may intervene by pre-teaching significant terms not mentioned by the students. After feeling comfortable that the class has adequately displayed their preexisting knowledge on the topic, they can be assigned the reading of the selection.

Reading Phase

During the reading, the students should be instructed to use the map as their guide to the major concepts. They may be asked to make either mental or graphic notes of information relevant to the categories displayed on the map. In this way, they know what to focus on while reading and what information is not pertinent to their purposes for reading.

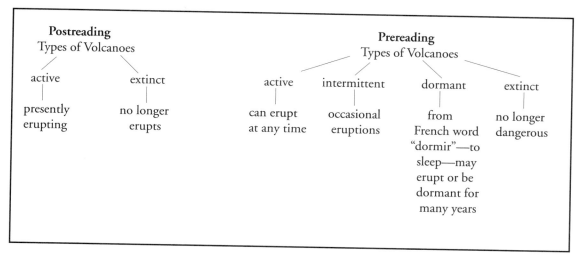

Postreading
Types of Volcanoes
- active
  - presently erupting
- extinct
  - no longer erupts

Prereading
Types of Volcanoes
- active
  - can erupt at any time
- intermittent
  - occasional eruptions
- dormant
  - from French word "dormir"—to sleep—may erupt or be dormant for many years
- extinct
  - no longer dangerous

Post-reading phase

Direct the attention of the class to the semantic map by asking them what new knowledge they gained about each of the categories. This new information should be added to the map until each major heading or category contains a cluster of topically related associations. The teacher may choose to use different shades of chalk or, if an overhead projector is used, different colors of transparency pens to illustrate the growth in knowledge before and after the reading. Note the changes in the students' knowledge base for the above example.

Questions can be asked to determine the depths of the students' understanding. To further extend the activity, have the students pose research questions which may lead them beyond the information presented in the selection read. For example, questions may arise such as "how do barnacles attach to ships?" (see "Arthropods," p. 68) or "What other mountains are in Alaska?" (see "Landforms" p. 66). Such probing can provide the impetus for interesting projects for library or community research.

As a stimulus for writing

Because semantic mapping presents the key concepts of a selection in an organized display, it is an excellent framework for a writing assignment. Working in pairs or small groups, students can be asked to choose a cluster of information on which to write. They may also be instructed to write about the overall topic (Landforms of the U. S., Arthropods, etc.), merging the concepts for each of the subcategories into separate paragraphs.

As with any new lesson, it is imperative that the writing assignment be thoroughly modeled at the onset. This can be accomplished by showing a completed paragraph and then enlisting the aid of the class in the composition of one or more sample paragraphs. Thus, the teacher is gradually releasing responsibility to the students before assigning independent practice.

As a review process

Semantic mapping can also be used exclusively in the post-reading phase as a means for reviewing the content of material just read or learned. The Algebra example (page 68) shows the strategy as it can be applied to a math review lesson on variables. In such an instance, the class is actively involved in the review process by contributing what they remember about a recent passage read or a lesson taught. The teacher aids this process by arranging the students' contributions in an organized manner.

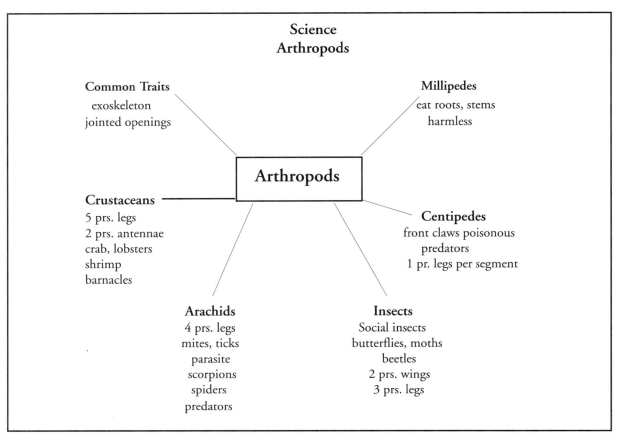

Science
Arthropods

Common Traits
  exoskeleton
  jointed openings

Millipedes
  eat roots, stems
  harmless

Arthropods

Crustaceans
5 prs. legs
2 prs. antennae
crab, lobsters
shrimp
barnacles

Centipedes
front claws poisonous
predators
1 pr. legs per segment

Arachids
4 prs. legs
mites, ticks
parasite
scorpions
spiders
predators

Insects
Social insects
butterflies, moths
beetles
2 prs. wings
3 prs. legs

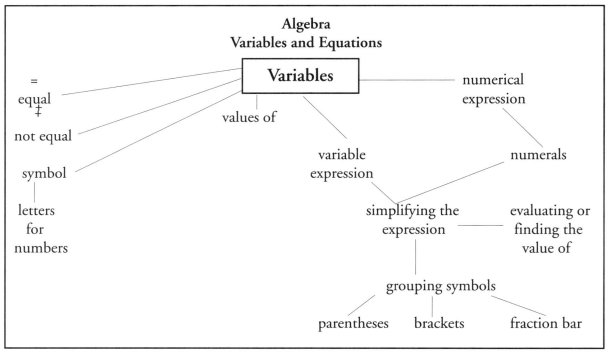

Algebra
Variables and Equations

Variables

=
equal
≠
not equal

symbol

letters
for
numbers

values of

numerical
expression

variable
expression

numerals

simplifying the
expression

evaluating or
finding the
value of

grouping symbols

parentheses   brackets   fraction bar

Summary

Semantic mapping represents a concept development approach to teaching vocabulary. Because students are actively involved in the process by contributing their preexisting knowledge on given topics, their interest is heightened, their knowledge base broadened, and their comprehension enhanced.

Perhaps by including in our repertoire of teaching strategies methods such as semantic mapping, the cliche "we teach as we were taught" may soon become a positive one. ♞

References

Davis, F.B. (1944). Fundamental factor of comprehension in reading. *Psychometrika, 9,* 185-187

Freedman, F.G., & Reynolds, E.G. (1980). Enriching basal reader lessons with semantic webbing. *The Reading Teacher, 33,* 677-684.

Hayes, D.A., & Tierney, R.J. (1982). Developing readers' knowledge through analogy. *Reading Research Quarterly, 17,* 256-280.

Johnson, D.D., & Pearson, P.D. (1984). *Teaching reading vocabulary,* Second Edition. New York: Holt, Rinehart and Winston.

Johnston, P., & Pearson P.D. (1982). Prior knowledge connectivity and the assessment of reading comprehension. Technical Report No. 245. Urbana, IL. University of Illinois,

Rumelhart, D.E., & Ortony, A. (1977). The representation of knowledge in memory. In R.C. Anderson, K.J. Spiro, & W.E. Montague (Eds.), *Schooling and the acquisition of knowledge.* Hillsdale, NJ: Lawrence Erlbaum.

Spiro, Rand J. (1977). Remembering information from text: The 'state of schema' approach. In R.C. Anderson, K.J. Spiro & W.E. Montague (Eds.), *Schooling and the acquisition of knowledge.* Hillsdale, NJ: Lawrence Erlbaum,

Swaby, B. (1984). FAN out your facts on the board. *The Reading Teacher, 37,* 914-16.

The job of the teacher is to make himself unnecessary
—Elbert Hubbard

What we want is to see the child in pursuit of knowledge
and not knowledge in pursuit of the child.
—George Bernard Shaw

How to integrate the communication processes with mathematics

The three strategies described here integrate reading, writing, listening, and speaking with the teaching and learning of mathematics.

The National Council of Teachers of Mathematics new *Curriculum and Evaluation Standards for School Mathematics* (NCTM, 1989) have included "the ability to communicate mathematics" among their five goals required to meet mathematics needs in the 21st century. Similarly, Steen (1989) has cited studies which suggest the need for full-scale revision of the mathematics curriculum. Among the actions called for are the need to a) *engage students* by making them active participants; b) *encourage teamwork* and *collaboration*; c) *encourage discussion*; and d) *require writing*, since it helps students learn to communicate about mathematics. Not only does writing help students clarify their own understanding, but for students who prefer written over quantitative expression, it provides a strategy more suited to their interests and abilities.

There is ample research support and numerous literature for incorporating writing instruction with the teaching of mathematics (Connolly & Vilardi, 1989; Davidson, 1977; Havens, 1989; Keith, 1988; Nahrang & Peterson, 1986; Noddings, 1985; Pearce & Davidson, 1989). A recent study by Smith, Grossman, and Miller (1990) has shown how integrating reading and writing can help students critically reflect about and apply new concepts. They maintain that students learn mathematics by reflecting on experience not just repetition of experience.

Included here are three strategies designed to increase students' conceptual knowledge of mathematics through the communication processes of reading, writing, listening, and speaking. Sample lessons are given which demonstrate the applicability of these techniques across grade levels and across topics in mathematics.

Paired or group retellings

Paired or group retellings (Wood, 1987) can be applied to mathematics to promote and practice the strategy of "talking aloud" the thought processes involved in computation and word problems. Although students can be grouped randomly as needed, it is more helpful to group them heterogeneously so that they can learn from their experiences and help one another.

Students grouped in threes could each be given a different computation problem on the same topic, for example, multiplying decimals. Each student must first solve the problem and either "think out loud" or write out the processes involved. Then one student can serve as facilitator to explain the processes used while pointing to each step in the problem. Other group members are free to confirm, refute, or add to the explanation given. Students can also be given the same problem to solve individually and then, with input from peers, discuss and embellish each other's retellings to discourage inadequate processing strategies.

Group Retellings
Mathematics—Sample Transcript
Decimals

Problem:	3.25 x .75=
Student A	First, we need to line up the numbers so we can multiply, without getting mixed up. 3.15 x.75
Student B	Then we start at the right and multiply like we usually would. Don't worry about the decimal right now.
Student C	5 5imes 5 is 25. The 5 goes under the 5's on the right and we carry the 2. Then multiply 5x1 which is 5, then add 2.
Student A	That's 7. And 5x3 is 15. That's 1575.
Student B	The next row moves over to the left one space. I get 2205. How about everybody else?
Student C	That's it. Now we add (pointing). Bring down the 5; 7 plus 5 is 12, carry the 1; 1 plus 5 is 6; 1 plus 2 is 3, and bring down the 2. That's 23625.
Student A	What about the decimal point?
Student B	Count the total number of digits to the right of the decimal in the problem—it's 4. Then start at the right of the answer and count 4 digits. The decimal goes to the left of the 4th digit.
Student C	So the answer is 2.3625!

Reaction guide

The reaction guide (Strategy 23) has been modified here to show its usefulness in mathematics (Wood, 1990). It consists of a series of five to eight statements which reflect general concepts about a topic. Students can work in pairs or small groups to find evidence to refute or confirm each statement. In mathematics, the reaction guide is useful as a review strategy to help students synthesize their understanding of important concepts. The guide shown on page 72 contains statements which are purposely incorrect. Students can talk aloud their thinking as they seek to determine the accuracy of the statements. They should be encouraged to refer to sample problems done in class or relevant pages in their text as well as relating the problems to everyday life.

Capsule vocabulary

Capsule Vocabulary (Crist, 1975) was developed as a follow-up to reinforce the vocabulary learned in a lesson, encourage participation from all class members, and promote communication skills. It is described in Strategy 7, but is applied only to language arts. The illustration on p. 72 demonstrates its applicability to mathematics as well. Students are given a list of key lesson terms or concepts (or they may brainstorm the concepts with input from the teacher). The teacher reviews the definitions of each term, relying on student input whenever possible and using the terms in a conversational manner. Next, working in pairs, students engage in a "conversational dialogue" using as many of the terms as possible. After about five minutes of discussion, pairs or groups of students compose a paper on the topic discussed, again using the key terms. It may be appropriate to impose a time limit for this writing activity to expedite the process. Groups may be asked to share their compositions with the rest of the class. Peer editing and evaluation is optional but not necessary since the primary purpose is to encourage written expression about concepts learned.

Reaction Guide

Mathematics
Points, Line Segments, and Angles—Review Lesson

Directions: With your partners or in your group, take turns reading and discussing each of the statements below. Put a check if you agree or disagree with each statement. Be sure to support your answer with at least one example. Use your book or any other sources for support.

1. All the points along an edge form a line segment.
   I agree __✔__   I disagree _____ because:

   in the baseball diamond shown on page 222 in our books, one line segment goes from 1st to 2l along this line segment.

2. Points can go on and on in one direction.
   I agree __✔__   I disagree _____ because:

   we learned that when they don't have two end points they are called rays. A ray can go on in one or both directions. endpoint •———→   *rays* ←———→

3. Line segments do not have to be straight; they can curve.
   I agree _____   I disagree __✔__ because:

   we learned that line segments go in different directions but they can't curve. p.23 shows that Path AC is a line segment, but AD isn't. A⌒C A⌐ D

4. The corners of the blackboard in our room do not form right angles.
   I agree _____   I disagree __✔__ because:

   when an angle is like a square corner, it is called a right angle. Blackboards have corners—so do our desks and the floors and walls in our room ⌐

5. The only reason we need to learn about lines, points, and angles is for school.
   I agree _____   I disagree __✔__ because

   for example, we need to know this information to measure length and distance— to build many things like houses, cars, and appliances.

Capsule Vocabulary
Mathematics
Metric Measures of Length

I. Present Vocabulary

meter	decimeter
kilometer	centimeter
hectometer	millimeter
dekameter	

II. Review definitions with student input:

Teacher: What does the prefix kilo tell us about the word kilometer?

Student A: kilo means 1,000

Student B: kilometer must be a thousand meters

Teacher: Suppose, the commercial said, "I'd walk a kilometer for a Camel." Would you walk more or less than a mile?

III. Students engage in conversational dialogue using vocabulary (in pairs):

Student A: Let's see, you'd measure the distance from my house to yours in kilometers.

Student B: And I guess you could measure the length of our driveway in dekameters.

Student A: …or maybe meters since a meter is a little longer than a yard.

IV. Students compose a paper on topic (pairs or small groups):

measuring length using the metric system is easy if you know that the <u>meter</u> is the basic unit of length and everything is based on 10. Just be careful not to confuse <u>centimeter</u> and <u>hectometer</u> or <u>decimeter</u> and <u>dekameter</u>. Remember, a <u>millimeter</u> is not a million meters; it's $\frac{1}{1000}$ of a meter. If you want to measure …

Summary

There is a growing emphasis throughout the nation to merge the communication processes of reading, writing, listening, speaking, and viewing with the teaching of subject matter. Shown here are three strategies designed to accomplish that goal which have the potential of increasing students' understanding of mathematics.

References

Connolly, P., & Vilardi, T. (1989). *Writing to learn mathematics and science.* New York: Columbia Teachers College Press.

Crist, B. (1975). One capsule a week: A painless remedy for vocabulary ills. *Journal of Reading, 19,* 147-149.

Davidson, J.E. (1977). The language experience approach to story problems. *Arithmetic Teacher, 25,* 28-30.

Havens, L. (1989). Writing to enhance learning in general mathematics. *Mathematics Teacher, 83,* 551-554.

Keith, S.Z. (1988). Explorative writing and learning mathematics. *Mathematics Teacher, 81,* 714-719.

Nahrgang, C.L., & Peterson, B.T. (1986). Using writing to learn mathematics. *Mathematics Teacher, 79,* 461-465.

National Council of Teachers of Mathematics. (1989). Curriculum and evaluation standards for school mathematics. Reston, VA: Author.

Noddings, N. (1985). Small groups as a setting for research on mathematical problem solving. In E. Silver (Ed.). *Teaching and learning mathematical problem solving: Multiple research perspectives,* Hillsdale, NJ: Lawrence Erlbaum.

Pearce, D.L., & Davidson, D.M. (1989). Language approach to mathematics instruction: Writing in the elementary classroom. *The Reading Professor, 11*(2), 8-12.

Smith, B., Grossman, F., & Miller, C. (1990). The integration of reading and writing in the teaching of mathematical concepts. Presentation for the College of Reading Association Annual Conference. Nashville, TN.

Steen, L.A. (1989). Teaching mathematics for tomorrow's world. *Educational Leadership, 47*(1), 18-22.

Wood, K.D. (1990). Collaborative strategies for improving students' conceptual understanding of mathematics. Presentation for the Macmillan Symposium on Mathematics and Science. Santa Fe, NM.

Wood, K.D. (1992). Meeting the social needs of adolescents through collaborative learning experiences. In J. Irvin (Ed.). *Transforming middle level education: Perspectives and possibilities.* New York: Allyn and Bacon.

How to teach writing as a process

Frames can make writing tasks much more manageable and usable in all subject areas.

The process-product controversy

Currently in the professional literature there is a philosophical debate between advocates of the process versus product approaches to teaching writing (King and Flitterman-King, 1986). Briefly, proponents of the product approach believe that if students receive direct instruction in the mechanics of writing (grammar, punctuation, syntax, spelling, etc.), the quality of their compositions will improve. In such an approach, students must seek information on a topic from encyclopedias, books, or other sources. Then they compose a paper, turn it in for credit and later receive a letter grade from the teacher. Only the teacher, not other students, has the opportunity to read the papers since the major emphasis is on the completion of the written product. Research by Brinon (1975) presents evidence confirming that such a procedure is normal practice when he observed that in 92% of the school writing assignments, the teacher was the sole audience.

Proponents of the process approach, on the other hand, encourage peer interaction and collaboration during the writing time. They allow for a prewriting period where initial thoughts and ideas are written down in preparation for the actual composition. Also, students are taught to write and revise more than one draft by sharing and editing each other's papers. The belief in this approach is that a polished essay requires much thought, revision, and peer input.

The process-product controversy is one reason offered for the fact that little writing practice takes place outside the English/Language Arts classroom (Goodlad 1983). Subject area teachers do not view themselves as purveyors of the rules of grammar and punctuation. Further, they are often devoid of meaningful, process-oriented strategies for incorporating writing with the teaching of subject matter. The notion of teacher writing then seems like an insurmountable chore.

Students who need assistance

When students need help in writing, instruction in the mechanical elements will be of little benefit, serving only to bore and frustrate them. Instead, they should have abundant opportunities to practice the process of writing by putting their thoughts in print. The National Assessment of Educational Progress Tests in Writing indicate that students' skills in the mechanics are much more advanced than their ability to write coherent, full-length passages.

Very often, students who lack proficient skills, have difficulty getting started and keeping focused on an issue when asked to respond in writing to a selection they have read. Therefore, this strategy, called paragraph or story frames (Fowler, 1982; Nichols, 1980), is designed to meet these needs. Paragraph and story frames are a sequence of spaces connected by key language elements. Paragraph frames are appropriate for content area texts whereas story frames (see Fowler, 1982 for more examples) are useful for narrative material. Story frames provide a structured format for students to follow to help them organize their thoughts on a given topic. Specifically, the frames provide the structure words (such as *next, finally, then*) which aid in the transition from one idea to another, thus giving students a framework for developing a logical, coherent piece of writing. Three examples depict a variety of frames which can be used as shown or modified by the teacher depending upon the lesson objectives. The fourth example (page 76) shows a sample frame using a seventh grade language arts lesson on a high-interest low reading level story called "Ghosts Don't Write Notes."

The strategy will be explained within the context of a model of direct instruction (excerpted from Blanton, Moorman and Wood, 1986) since such models are being adhered to in our schools as part of the recent emphasis on effective teaching. Using the term direct instruction in conjunction with the teaching of writing as a process may sound somewhat paradoxical. However, much of what

Character analysis
(Nichols, 1980)

In the story _____
by _____ the major character is
_____ who is _____
Another main character is _____.
The problem which the major character faces is that _____
_____
_____
The story ends with _____
The lesson I learned from reading this story was that _____
_____

Essay: Time Order
(Nichols, 1980)

At the end of _____ what happened
was that _____
Previous to this _____
_____
Before this _____
The entire chain of events had begun for a number of reasons
including _____.
Some prominent incidents which helped to trigger the conflict
were _____

Essay: Comparison-contrast
(Nichols, 1980)

_____ are different from _____
in several ways. First of all _____
while _____
Secondly, _____
while _____
In addition, _____
while _____
So it should be evident that _____
_____

is advocated by process proponents lends itself well to such a model, given that the development of writing proficiency, like any skill, requires explication, modeling, and guided practice.

Procedures

I. *Modeling Strategies.* As with any new strategy or concept, frames should be modeled by the teacher before being used individually. This may entail a number or modeling sessions with one type of frame applied to several different selections.

1) Begin by explaining the process of the lesson to the entire class. The purpose in this instance would be to help students organize their thoughts, into a logical, written form.

2) Display the frame before reading (or listening) to the story. This can be accomplished via an overhead projector or the blackboard.

3) Tell the students to read (or listen) to a sample selection with the framework in mind. The frame then provides them with a purpose for reading (or listening) .

4) The students, with the aid of the teacher, fill in each line of the frame. Be prepared to narrow the focus of their responses since initially they may be inclined to trail off into an abundance of unnecessary details. Also, although numerous responses may be possible, encourage the students to reach a consensus on the information to be included.

5) Allow students to volunteer to read the completed story frame orally. Have them evaluate the finished product to determine if it adequately reflects the events in the selection and if it requires additional revision stylistically.

II. *Guided Practice.* The guided practice stage is necessary to determine if students have mastered the concept being taught. Here, under the teacher's guidance, they can practice their writing and share their experience with peers.

6) Assign a selection (preferably from the students' textbooks) to be read either silently or orally. (Reading orally can be done in pairs at a low volume.)

7) Permit students to work in pairs or small groups to produce one common frame.

8) Students then can take turns reading and editing their completed frames. After the final editing, the finished products are turned in to the teacher for credit and/or classroom displays.

III. *Independent Application.*

9) After modeling and practicing various frames, and when the teacher feels the students understand the concept, frames can be assigned as an independent activity. Various frames can be repro-

duced and placed in an easily accessible area in the classroom. Students can read selections (either assigned or self-selected) and fill in the appropriate frame. These completed frames must be shared and edited by a partner before being turned in for credit.

A Final Note

The use of story or paragraph frames is beneficial for a number of reasons: 1) they promote and channel peer interaction in a productive manner; 2) they help students lacking in writing proficiency to focus their ideas; 3) they provide a means for subject area teachers to incorporate writing practice with their instructional lesson; and 4) they make the task of writing more manageable for both the teacher and the students. 🐎

References

Blanton, W. E., Moonnan, G. B., & Wood, K.D.(1986, December). A model of direct instruction applied to the basal skills lesson. *The Reading Teacher, 40,* pp. 299-305.

Brinon, J. et al.(1975). *The development of writing abilities.* London, England: Macmillan Education.

Fowler, G. L.(1982, November). Developing comprehension skills in primary students through the use of story frames. *The Reading Teacher, 36,* pp. 176-179

Goodlad, J.I. (1983). *A place called school* New York: McGraw-Hill.

King, D. C., & Fluterman-King, S.(1986, December). The tug-of-war is on between writing approaches: Emphasis on process challenges the five paragraph essay. *Association for Supervision and Curriculum Development Curriculum Update.*

Nichols, J. N. (1980, December). Using paragraph frames to help remedial high school students with writing assignments. *Journal of Reading, 24,* pp. 228-231.

To seek and find a method by which the teachers teach less and learners learn more.
—John Amos Comenius, 1650

Personally I'm always ready to learn, although I do not always like being taught.
—Winston Churchill

How to help students remember what they read

Showing students how to put information in their own words, called self-recitation or verbal rehearsal, is a very powerful study technique.

The act of verbal rehearsal, reciting information to ourselves using our own words is a universal phenomenon. Everyone engages in this process and we do so on a daily basis. We mentally or subvocally review the day's agenda while driving in our cars; we go over important addresses or phone numbers in our heads; or we repeat aloud the directions to a location we are trying to reach. All of these efforts are engaged in for the purpose of remembering or retelling information.

Not surprisingly, verbal rehearsal has a place in the classroom as well. We can engage in verbal rehearsal, or self-recitation, in three ways: 1) orally, talking aloud to ourselves or another person; 2) graphically, writing down information in our own words; or 3) mentally, reviewing content in our heads. The graphic representation of self-recitation typically comes up under the heading of summary writing.

According to Pauk (1974), self-recitation is the most powerful study technique available. Empirical research supports that claim suggesting that summarizing is a valuable study strategy which seems to improve recall, retention, and comprehension (Bretzing and Kulhavy, 1979; Devine, 1991; Palincsar and Brown, 1983; Taylor, 1992).

What follows is a description of a model for teaching students how to recast information in their own words both orally and graphically. This is followed by a description of a procedure called hierarchical summary writing (Taylor, 1992) which shows how to apply this ability to the study of textbook content. Lastly, a framework for writing sequential summaries with expository text is provided (Hill, 1991).

Modeling the process

Koskinen, Gambrell, Kapinus, and Heathington (1988) have suggested a model for teaching students how to put information in their own words. The following sequence is adapted from their recommendations:

1. *Explain the purpose and rationale*

Ask students if they have ever had any difficulty remembering what they read or hear. Explain that one of the best ways to remember is to recite the content, using their own language as much as possible. Use everyday examples of how they might tell a friend about a movie or trip and how the first retelling of the event makes recall easier the next time. Explain that they will learn a strategy to help them know how to retell information.

2. *Model and demonstrate*

Begin by reading aloud a brief passage of approximately 50 to 100 words. Using actual textbook selections is most beneficial here. An overhead projector can be used to provide students with a visual stimulus as well. Then retell the content in two to three sentences. Talk aloud the thinking used in order to make the process more concrete and understandable. A sample teacher dialogue might be: "As I read the selection to you about making silk, listen for the important ideas. Then, I will retell the passage using my own words."

3. *Sample Passage:*

Making Silk: Silk comes from silkworms which hatch from the eggs of a large white moth. They eat a great many mulberry leaves daily. After a month or so, the worms are fully grown. They begin to make themselves a covering, called a cocoon. Many caterpillars do the same thing, but the cocoons of silkworms are made of a long silk thread. The cocoons are then sold to silk factories. People in factories work with millions of cocoons to turn them into silk threads, then into cloth. Silk cloth is very beautiful. What makes it so costly is the long time and great care that go into making it.

Teacher: "Now, I will retell the story without looking back to the original passage."

Silkworms hatch from moth eggs and begin to eat mulberry leaves every day. In a month, they grow and make a cocoon of silk thread which is sold to silk factories. There, the silk threads are turned into expensive cloth.

Teacher: How did I do? Did I include the main points?

The students may contribute other ideas at this point.

Guided practice

The guided practice portion of the instructional sequence is most effective when it proceeds from a whole class, small group, paired to individual practice paradigm. For example, the teacher can provide another passage on the overhead and ask the class as a whole to retell the content. The class-generated retelling can also be written on the transparency.

Next, students can be grouped in fours or fives (or pairs) to engage in communal writing of a selection retelling (see Strategy 7 for communal writing). If additional practice is deemed necessary, the students can work in pairs to practice the summarizing/retelling process.

Independent practice

Students can then be instructed to write their retellings individually as they read portions of their textbook. This is similar to the hierarchal summary writing described next.

Transfer and application

Make students aware that retelling can aid them in understanding and remembering material both in and out of school. They also need to know that they can engage in silent verbal rehearsal, retelling information in their head (rather than writing it down) whenever they want to ensure retention.

Hierarchical summary writing

Taylor (1992) has used what she terms hierarchical summaries with much success. In this technique students summarize in writing the most important ideas from a textbook selection. They read one section at a time, proceeding from one heading to the next, and writing the most important ideas about the topic. Their summaries should be limited to two or three sentences, if possible. The model for retelling described previously provides excellent preparation for this procedure.

Hill (1991), for example, began by teaching students to recount events chronologically before proceeding to more abstract summary writing such as cause-effect, compare-contrast, or problem-solution. The following example shows how the sequential pattern frame can be used as students summarize a social studies passage .

After summarizing the assigned selection, students review what they have written, reciting the content in their own words. In this way, the actual textbook heading alone provide the stimulus for review. Shown above is an example of a hierarchical summary for a chapter in a health textbook.

Sequential summary writing

Several studies have reported success when a narrative chronology, in most cases a time order sequence, was applied to expository material (Hill, 1991; Pincus, Geller and Stover, 1986; Taylor, 1986). In general, these researchers' findings suggest that a) summary writing is most effective if it begins with a narrative organization since it is most familiar to students, and b) enumeration and sequential formats with text frames prove to be successful.

A Final Note

Merely giving students the assignment to retell a selection in their own words and write a summary is insufficient. On the contrary, reviews of the research have indicated that summarizing information is only effective if it has been thoroughly modeled and demonstrated (Anderson and Ambruster, 1984; Devine, 1991; Hill, 1991). ♞

References

Anderson, T.H., & Armbruster, B.B. (1984). Studying. In P.D. Pearson (Ed.), *Handbook of reading research,* pp. 657-679. New York: Longman.

Bretzing, B.B., & Kulhavy, R.W. (1979). Notetaking and depth of processing. *Contemporary Educational Psychology, 4,* 145-153.

Devine, T.G. (1991). Studying: Skills, strategies and systems. In J. Flood, J.M. Jensen, D. Lapp, & J.R. Squine (Eds.), *Handbook of research on teaching the English language arts* (pp. 743-753). New York: Macmillan.

Hill, M. (1991). Writing summaries promotes thinking and learning across the curriculum—but why are they so difficult to write? *Journal of Reading, 34,* 536-539.

Koskinen, P.S., Gambrell, L.B., Kapinus, B.A., & Heathington, B.S. (1988). Retelling: A strategy for enhancing students' reading comprehension. *The Reading Teacher, 41,* 892-896.

Palincsar, A.S., & Brown, A.L. (1983). *Reciprocal teaching of comprehension monitoring activities* (Technical Report No. 269). Champaign, Illinois, Center for the Study of Reading (ERIC Document Reproduction Service No. ED 225 135)

Pauk, W. (1974). *How to study in college.* Boston: Houghton Mifflin.

Pincus, A., Geller, E.B., & Stover, E.M. (1986). A technique for using story schema as a transition to understanding and summarizing event based magazine articles. *Journal of Reading, 30,* 152-158.

Taylor, B.M. (1992). Text structure, comprehension, and recall. In S.J. Samuels & A.E. Farstrup (Eds.), *What research has to say about reading instruction,* (pp. 220-235). Newark, DE: International Reading Association.

Taylor, B.M. (1986). Teaching middle grade students to summarize content textbook material. In J.F. Baumann (Ed.), *Teaching main idea comprehension,* pp. 195-209 . Newark, DE: International Reading Association.

I hear and I forget
I see and I remember
I do and I understand.
—Chinese proverb

How to promote lifelong readers across the curriculum

Practical and easy to implement methods to encourage students to read for pleasure and information are described here.

According to data from the National Assessment of Educational Progress in Reading our nations' students tend to be infrequent readers. At all three ages assessed (9, 13, 17), approximately one-fifth of the students reported reading for pleasure only yearly or never. Fewer than half the students reported having engaged in the following activities including telling a friend about a book, taking a book out of the library, spending their own money on books, and reading more than one book by a favorite author (Mullis, 1992).

While the promotion of reading for pleasure is typically viewed as the domain of the reading/language arts teacher, the responsibility can and should be shared across the curriculum by teachers of all subject areas. Incorporating literature with subject area instruction can be an enriching experience for teachers and students alike without the burden of an added responsibility. Answers to questions teachers typically pose about using literature across the curriculum are provided here.

How can I encourage students to read for pleasure?

A number of factors contribute to successful experiences in a literature-oriented classroom. Among these factors are the following:

a) *Create an atmosphere conducive to reading.*
Middle level teachers can create in their classrooms an atmosphere that invites and encourages reading. Teachers have reported an increased interest in reading when a special corner of the room is established with such comforts as a rug, a reading lamp, bean bag chairs or a plant (Clary, 1991). In addition, the corner of the room, in general, can be enhanced by displaying colorful posters (some bookstores are willing to release these after a promotion), mobiles, book jackets, and examples of students' written or artistic work.

b) *Make books available.* When books are accessible and attractively displayed, students will tend to read more frequently (Clary, 1991). Having a lot of books displayed in a classroom immediately communicates to students that this is a class where reading is important. The books should be appropriate for a wide range of reading abilities, reflect varied genres (fiction, nonfiction, poetry, plays) and may or may not be topically related to current instruction. In addition, frequent reading aloud to students (yes, even in the middle grades!) is another way to capture the attention of all ability levels.

c) *Allow students to self-select their books.* While many reading experiences may be teacher-assigned, allowing students to choose their selections can be very motivating. Some teachers may feel anxious about the self-selection process, yet as readers gain experience in reading for pleasure, they tend to select more appropriate materials (Nell, 1988). Students can be taught from the beginning of the year that the reward for finishing an assignment early is not more work but rather the opportunity to read their self-selected book.

d) *Make time for reading.* There are a number of strategies described in the professional literature to give students time for reading such as DEAR (Drop Everything and Read), SQUIRT (Sustained Quiet Reading Time), USSR (Uninterrupted Sustained Silent Reading), to cite a few. Although the names are different, these strategies are similar in that they recommend 15 minutes or more of daily reading time and modeling by the teacher and other adults. Many teachers have found that random rather than scheduled reading time serves as both a reward and a means to focus students' attention.

Where can I find appropriate literature?

The first resource a classroom teacher should consider is the school media specialist. In addition, there are many published sources available which provide informative annotations of each selection.

Sources for Literature in the Middle Grades

ALAN Review. Assembly on Literature for Adolescents. National Council of Teachers of English (published 3 times a year).

Appraisal: Science Books for Young People. Children's Science Book Review Committee (Published 3 times a year).

Carlsen, G. R. (1980). *Books and the Teenage Reader (2nd ed.)* New York: Harper and Row.

Donelson, K., & Nilsen, A. P. (1985). *Literature for Todays Young Adults (2nd ed.)* Glenview, IL: Scott Foresman.

Dreyer, S. (1977; 1981; 1987). *The Bookfinder: A Guide to Children's Literature About the Needs and Problems of Youth Aged 2-15.* Circle Pines, NM: American Guidance Service.

Monson, D. (1985). *Adventuring with Books.* Urbana, IL: National Council of Teachers of English.

Reed, A. J. S. (1988). *Comics to Classics: A Parent's Guide to Books for Teens and Preteens.* Newark, DE: International Reading Association.

Teens' Favorite Books: Young Adult Choices 1987-1992 (1992). Newark, DE: International Reading Association.

How can I relate the literature to my instruction?

Using the sources listed previously, teachers can make certain that various books on a topic are readily accessible in their classrooms. A cart of books from the library can be wheeled in at the start of a unit. Then, in order to entice the students and assist them with their choices, the teacher, media specialist or fellow students may even choose to conduct brief book-talks. Such book-talks can be entertaining and entice students to read the books displayed (Bodart, 1985). Notice that the selections below include a combination of fiction and nonfiction. While none are listed here, poetry and plays are additional types of literature which can be included in the thematic unit.

Literature selections on various topics

History:
The American Revolution
O'Dell, S. *Sarah Bishop*
Forbes, E. *Johnny Tremain*
Collier, J. & Collier, C. *The Bloody Country*
Campion, N. R. *Patrick Henry: Firebrand of the Revolution*
Meltzer, M. *The American Revolutionaries: A History in Their Own Words*
Davis, B. *Heroes of the American Revolution*

Language Arts:
Working together/Collaboration
Voigt, C. *Dicey's Song*
Brooks, B. *The Moves Make the Man*
Frank, A. *The Diary of a Young Girl*
Hunt, I. *Across Five Aprils*
George, J. C. *Julie of the Wolves*
Lowry, L. *Number the Stars*
Ballard, R. D. *Exploring the Titanic*

Health/Science/Language Arts:
Death/dying
Carter, A. R. *Shelia's Dying*
Lowry, L. *A Summer to Die*
O'Brien, R. *Z for Zachariah*
Craven, C. M. *I Heard the Owl Call MY Name*
Bennett, J. *The Haunted One*

How can I keep track of my students' reading?

Most teachers want to find some way to manage self-selected or assigned reading in their classrooms. Fortunately, with the increased emphasis on the reading/writing connection and cross-curricular integration, the traditional book report is rapidly becoming extinct. In its place are a number of exciting alternatives including dialogue journals, art projects, dramatic activities, book-talks, critiques (kept on file in the media center), and mock book videos, to name a few.

A Reader Response Form (modified from Wood and Mason, 1981) helps students see the range of responses from which to choose and helps teachers keep a record of their book and response choices. One section of the form asks if the student completed the book. Some students feel compelled to read any book they have started. Others may begin reading a chapter or two, feel it is not worth completing and will make another choice. Such a reaction should be accepted and a brief, critical analysis written on the form. The teacher may choose to give partial credit for such an endeavor.

Reader Response Form

Name _____ Class _____ Date _____

Title of Book _____

Author _____

I chose this book because _____

Number of pages: _____

I read the entire book: _____ yes _____ no

I read the book: _____ at home _____ at school _____ both

Reaction to the book: (Circle a number):

I liked it very much 5

I liked it 4

It was okay 3

I disliked it 2

I disliked it very much. 1

Indicate the way you want to respond to this book or check with your teacher for a possible recommendation. With the exception of your journal entry, attach your response to this form.

_____	Card file critique	_____	If I could change one thing about the book it would be…
_____	Synopsis	_____	After reading this book, I learned…
_____	Take a position on an issue in the book	_____	Book review
_____	Blurb	_____	Book conference with teacher
_____	My favorite part(s) is/are	_____	Conduct a book-talk for the class or group
_____	My favorite character(s) is/are	_____	This book reminds me of …
_____	Write a letter to a friend	_____	I was puzzled by …
_____	Design a book jacket	_____	Write in my journal (free response)
_____	Describe an experience from the perspective of a character or thing in the book	_____	Write a skit, play

Samples of previous student work or teacher-designed examples may be used as models for each of the options listed. The teacher may also choose to model a response variation such as a book jacket blurb and require that the entire class write one to coordinate with a pre-assigned selection. More than one reader response to each book may also be required or encouraged. For example, students might write a personal response about the book in their journals and afterwards develop a card file critique, or write a book review or design a skit with peers.

A form such as this one (used previously by this author as a teacher in the middle school) can serve as a means to keep track of and give credit for students' reading. It is especially useful for subject area teachers who want to incorporate reading and writing across the curriculum but may not be familiar or comfortable with the many alternatives to the traditional book report. Of course, the form can and should be modified to coordinate with each teacher's academic objectives.

It is recommended that grading of such responses be kept to a minimum. Instead encourage peer sharing and assistance if deemed necessary. Remember, the primary objective is to reward and encourage reading as much as possible. With commitment from teachers across the curriculum, the promotion of lifelong reading habits can begin, not end, in the middle grades. ♞

References

Bodart-Talbot, J. (1985). *Book talk 2: Book talking for all ages and audiences.* New York: H. W. Wilson.

Clary, L. (1991). Getting adolescents to read. *Journal of Reading 34,* 340-345.

Mullis, I. (1992) *NAEP Facts: Trends in school and home contexts for learning.* U. S. Department of Education, Office of Educational Research and Improvement.

Nell, V. (1988). *Lost in a book: The psychology of reading for pleasure.* New Haven, CT: Yale University Press.

Wood, K. D., & Mason, G. (1981). Making individualized reading feasible in the content areas. *Journal of Reading, 25,* 167.

We should not only use the brains we have, but all that we can borrow.
—Woodrow Wilson

If we would have new knowledge,
we must get a whole world of new questions.
—Suzanne K. Langer

How to help students comprehend their textbooks

Using a textbook activity guide can help students focus on the most significant information.

Recent research in cognitive psychology has emphasized metacognition and its effect on students' comprehension. Baker and Brown (1984a) define metacognition as "awareness of the skills and strategies needed to perform a learning task effectively and the ability to use these strategies selectively."

According to Baker and Brown (1984), while the term metacognition is new to professional literature, the concepts underlying its use have been espoused since the time of Dewey and Thorndike. Students who possess sound metacognitive abilities, while reading, continually relate their prior knowledge to new information in the text, predict what might occur next, reread when something fails to make sense, evaluate the content of what was read, engage in self-questioning, and focus only on the significant portions of the text. All of these strategies, while often performed automatically, lead to a clearer understanding of written material.

On the other hand, students who lack these metacognitive skills, the poor comprehenders, tend to read slowly and laboriously at the same rate of speed, often failing to use corrective strategies when something does not make sense. Thus for the good comprehenders, reading is an active, dynamic process involving interaction with the print, whereas,

for the poor comprehenders, reading is a passive activity involving minimal reader involvement.

Since most middle level classrooms are single textbook classrooms, and given the fact that teachers can expect to find a range of reading abilities, spanning from six to ten grade levels or more (Singer and Donlan, 1980), it becomes obvious that many students will have difficulty comprehending the textbooks intended for their grade level. Merely assigning the reading of a textbook chapter and asking students to complete the end-of-chapter questions only exacerbates the problem of the poor comprehenders. In such instances, students do not find out what their purposes for reading are until they reach the final questions. Then they must attempt to reread in order to effectively retrieve the information requested. By this time, they are often frustrated, bewildered, and, in some cases, hostile about the assignment given.

In view of these problems, what can the teacher do to address the needs of the poor comprehenders? One solution is to design study guides to accompany the more difficult chapters in the textbook.

Study guides are advantageous for two reasons. First, they enable the teacher to reduce the amount of print students must deal with at a given time by using questions interspersed throughout the text rather than relying on the author-constructed, end-of-chapter questions. Secondly, these guides can be developed to aid students' metacognitive abilities while they read the text. As such, study guides serve as "tutors in print form" (Wood and Mateja, 1983) to help students vary their reading rate, monitor their comprehension, and focus on the most significant information.

A variety of study guides have been described in the literature including Cunningham and Shablak's (1975) guide-o-rama, Vacca's (1981) description of concept and pattern guides, and Herber's (1978) three level guide. The textbook activity guide or TAG (Davey, 1986) which is designed specifically to improve students' metacognitive skills is described here.

Procedures for developing a TAG

The following procedures are necessary for developing a textbook activity guide:

1) Select a portion of a textbook chapter which typically causes students some difficulty. Decide upon the significant concepts and determine the appropriate task for each concept. Davey (1986) suggests using semantic maps or diagrams when it is necessary to organize information, or promoting discussion between two or more students when a critical analysis is required.

2) Develop both a strategy code and a self monitoring code to assist students in the metacognitive process. The use of these codes should be thoroughly modeled and explained to the students. Then, make certain that they are printed at the top of each guide for easy reference. Sample codes modified somewhat from Davey, follow:

Strategy Codes

RR   Read and retell in your own words, taking turns with your partner.

PP   Predict with your partner.

WR   Provide a written response on your own and compare with your partner.

Skim   Look at the purpose stated and read quickly. Afterwards, discuss with your partner.

MOC Develop a semantic map, outline, or chart with your partner which depicts the information in this section.

Self-monitoring Codes

\-   I understood this information

?   I'm not certain if I understand.

x   I do not understand and I need to restudy.

3) Design a guide which reflects your chapter objectives and which is appropriate for the majority of students in your classroom.

Using the TAG in the classroom

1) Thoroughly explain, model, and demonstrate the strategy and self-monitoring codes by walking students through their first TAG. Discuss how it is necessary to vary one's reading rate to avoid laboriously reading every word. Help them to see how and when to use corrective strategies (e.g. rereading, skipping a section, and reading ahead to gather more information, etc.) when something does not seem logical.

2) Then assign each student a partner. Pairing a student with someone who is slightly more proficient in reading can be advantageous for both learners.

3) Monitor the progress of each day by circulating around the room to offer assistance and maintain the pacing of the lesson. At this point it is helpful to check students' self-monitoring codes to determine if additional clarification is necessary.

4) After completion engage the students in a discussion of the guide questions by asking them to show what information in the text led them to that answer.

5) Lastly, help students become aware of how these readings/study strategies should be internalized and applied to other settings even when a guide is not available.

To further illustrate the classroom application of this strategy a sample guide from an eighth grade science chapter dealing with fossils is shown followed by a guide for a seventh grade social studies textbook on countries of the Persian Gulf and Arabia.

Textbook Activity Guide
Modern Earth Science
Holt, Rinehart and Winston, 1983
Topic: Fossils

Names _____ Date(s) _____

_____

Strategy Codes:

RR	Read and retell in your own words
DP	Read and discuss with partner
PP	Predict with partner
WR	Write a response on your own
Skim	Read quickly for purpose stated and discuss with partner
MOC	Organize information with a map, chart, or outline

Self-monitoring Codes:

___	I understand this information
_?_	I'm not sure if I understand
_x_	I do not understand and I need to restudy

1. ___ PP pp. 385-391. Survey the title, picture, charts, and headings
   What do you expect to learn about this section?

2. ___ WR As you are reading, jot down three or more new words and definitions for your vocabulary collection.

3. ___ RR pp. 385-6 first three paragraphs

4. ___ DP pp. 386-7 next three paragraphs.
   a. Describe several reasons why index or guide fossils are important.
   b. How can finding the right type of fossil help you to identify it?

5. ___ MOC Map pp. 387-9. Make an outline of the information.

6. ___ Skim p. 390 first three paragraphs
   Purpose: To understand the role of the following in the formation of fossils
   ___ a. natural casts   ___ b. trails and burrows   ___ c. gastroliths

7. ___ DP pp. 390-1. As an amateur fossil collector describe:
   a. where to find fossils; b. what to use to find them; c. how to prepare them for display

8. ___ WR p. 392 next to last paragraph. Define pseudofossil. Jot down three other words which contain the prefix "pseudo." Use the dictionary if necessary.

9. ___ DP Examine the fossil collection being passed around and list eight things you have learned by analyzing it.

Textbook Activity Guide
The African and Asian World
Macmillan Publishing Co., Inc., 1983
Topic: Countries of the Persian Gulf and Arabia

1. ___ DP pp. 139-150. *Before* surveying the text with your partner, brainstorm about your existing knowledge on this topic. Jot down your ideas. Compare your responses *after* surveying the text.

2. ___ WR Jot down five or more vocabulary words and definitions for your collection

3. ___ DP pp. 139-40. In your own words, what are the five common characteristics of these countries?

4. ___ Skim p. 140. How has oil caused conflict and change?

5. ___ WR p. 140-1 —Iraq. Name three major facts you learned about Iraq.

6. ___ RR p. 141-2—Agriculture. Briefly summarize your retellings.

7. ___ DP pp. 142-4—Oil. How has oil production influenced life in Iraq?

8. ___ MOC p. 143. Refer to the map at the bottom of p. 143. Make a graph depicting the major industry and resources in these countries.

9. ___ DP pp. 144-5—Iran. React to the following and substantiate your responses.
   a. The Iranians welcomed foreigners.
   b. Khomeini favored progress and an emphasis on new technology.

10. ___ RR pp. 146. After reading and retelling, synthesize your knowledge about a) land reform, b) productive lands, and c) manufacturing.

11. ___ MOC p. 146-8—Saudi Arabia. Make a chart comparing and contrasting the two groups in Saudi Arabia, the hadan and the badia.

12. ___ DP p. 148-150. a. Write down some facts about the Arabian Peninsula (Also, refer to map on p. 134. b. What is the role of sheiks? c. How did oil production change Saudi Arabia?

13. ___- MOC p. 150. After referring to the map on p. 134 and reading this section outline the three sections of the Arabian Borderlands.

Summary

Although described here as a strategy largely for use with below average comprehenders, textbook activity guides can be useful for students of varied ability levels who are not yet proficient in sound reading and study habits. Research by this author (Wood, 1986) has indicated that good readers receive much benefit from using questions interspersed throughout text. As students become more knowledgeable about the strategies needed to effectively comprehend international text, the use of study guides can be eliminated for selected individuals. In this way, the teacher gradually releases responsibility for comprehending to the students who, with guidance and practice, can now assimilate these metacognitive abilities into their daily reading. ♞

References

Baker, L., & Brown, A.L. (1984a). Cognitive monitoring in reading. In James Flood. (Ed.), *Understanding reading comprehension* Newark, DE: International Reading Association.

Baker, L., & Brown, A.L. (1984). Metacognitive skills and reading. In P. David Pearson (Ed.) *Handbook of reading research.* New York: Longman Inc.

Cunningham, D,. & Shablak, S.L. (1975). Selective reading guide-o-rama: The content teacher's best friend. *Journal of Reading, 18*

Davey, B. (1986). Using textbook activity guides to help students learn from textbooks. *Journal of Reading, 29.* 489-494.

Herber, H.L. (1978). *Teaching reading in the content areas* Englewood Cliffs, NJ.: Prentice-Hall.

Singer, H., & Donlan, D. (1980). *Reading and learning fromtext.* Boston: Little, Brown,

Vacca, R.T. (1981). *Content area reading.* Boston: Little, Brown,

Wood, K.D., & Mateja, J.A. (1983). Adapting secondary level strategies for use in elementary classrooms. *The Reading Teacher, 36,* 492-497.

Wood, K.D. (1986). The effect of interspersing questions in text: Evidence for slicing the task. *Reading Research and Instruction, 25,* 295-307.

How to guide students through the reading of subject area material

The Reading Road Map is an effective way to help students gain more information from their subject area textbooks.

Research has clearly shown that the textbook is the predominant source for over ninety percent of the instruction in classrooms today (EPIE, 1977; Goodlad, 1976). This dependence on the textbook begins in the primary grades and increases with each advancing grade (Goodlad, 1976). Research has also shown that the textbooks used in our schools are not particularly well-written (Armbruster and Anderson, 1981). Armbruster (1984) uses the concept of "inconsiderate text" to describe those textbooks and passages which violate principles of effective learning. Textbooks can be labeled **inconsiderate** when a sequence of events is presented inconsistently, referents are unclear, or signaling devices such as titles, subheadings or topic sentences are illogically structured. Another indicator of a poorly written textbook is the kind of question typically appearing at the end of sections or chapters.

Armbruster's research has revealed that the overwhelming majority of questions found in fifth grade social studies textbooks, for example, asked for details which require identification of names, dates and definitions. Very few questions were of the main idea type which would require that students focus on the most significant concepts and events. When these end-of-chapter questions are the predominant assignment given, students attend to the less important information presented in the text and emerge with little or no conceptual understanding of the content.

One way to guide students through the reading of informational or subject area text is through the use of interspersed questions designed to coordinate with the topics and headings. In this approach, questions are sequentially presented and students answer them while they read through the textbook selection. In a typical textbook chapter where the questions appear at the end, the students do not know what information is deemed important until after they have finished reading the assignment. Teachers can intervene in this process by developing a reading guide, a strategy designed to intersperse questions throughout the text selection instead of saving them all until the end. In this way, the students see what the teacher, not the textbook publisher, thinks is important in the chapter.

Numerous types of reading or study guides have been reported in the professional literature including the learning-from-text-guide (Singer and Donal, 1980), the guide-o-rama (Cunningham and Shablak, 1975), concept and pattern guides (Vacca, 1981), the three level guide (Herber, 1970) and the textbook activity guide (Davey, 1986), to name a few. Described here is a new version of the reading guide called the Reading Road Map (Wood, 1988).

Reading Road Map
Chapter 22
Canada

SKIM GUIDE 1st		READ AND WRITE 2nd
LOCATION	SPEED	MISSION

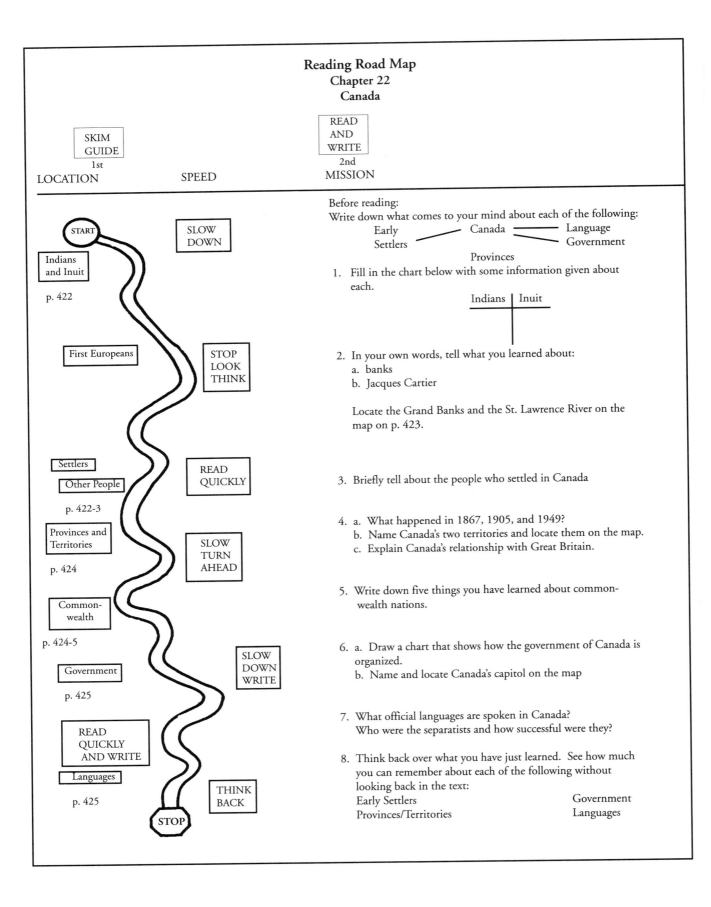

START

Indians and Inuit
p. 422

SLOW DOWN

First Europeans

STOP LOOK THINK

Settlers
Other People
p. 422-3

READ QUICKLY

Provinces and Territories
p. 424

SLOW TURN AHEAD

Common-wealth
p. 424-5

Government
p. 425

SLOW DOWN WRITE

READ QUICKLY AND WRITE

Languages
p. 425

THINK BACK

STOP

Before reading:
Write down what comes to your mind about each of the following:
Early Settlers — Canada — Language / Government
Provinces

1. Fill in the chart below with some information given about each.

    Indians | Inuit

2. In your own words, tell what you learned about:
    a. banks
    b. Jacques Cartier

    Locate the Grand Banks and the St. Lawrence River on the map on p. 423.

3. Briefly tell about the people who settled in Canada

4. a. What happened in 1867, 1905, and 1949?
    b. Name Canada's two territories and locate them on the map.
    c. Explain Canada's relationship with Great Britain.

5. Write down five things you have learned about common-wealth nations.

6. a. Draw a chart that shows how the government of Canada is organized.
    b. Name and locate Canada's capitol on the map

7. What official languages are spoken in Canada?
    Who were the separatists and how successful were they?

8. Think back over what you have just learned. See how much you can remember about each of the following without looking back in the text:
    Early Settlers   Government
    Provinces/Territories   Languages

The Reading Road Map helps students read a passage at different speeds to coordinate with the different purposes for reading. A chapter introduction or summary, for example, need not be read as conscientiously as a description of the causes of volcanic eruptions. While good readers subconsciously know when to skim over material which is not significant, less proficient readers tend to read all textual material at the same rate—often either very slowly and laboriously or very quickly and carelessly.

Through the use of "road signs" to depict the speed, the Reading Road Map helps students know when to vary their reading speed. Shown is a Reading Road Map for a middle level social studies textbook. This guide demonstrates how students journey through the text using missions (interspersed questions), road signs (reading rate indicators) and location signs (headings, page numbers, etc.)

Designing the guide

Begin by deciding on the most significant information in the textbook chapter or selection. Then, proceed sequentially by designing questions, activities, or statements which emphasize the significant concepts. Notice how the guide begins with a question designed to elicit students prior knowledge. Since prior knowledge is a major contributor to comprehension, the addition of such an activity helps to establish a firm foundation of previous experience from which to begin the new "journey." Notice, too, how the map concludes with an associational activity designed to encourage a mental review of the recently encountered concepts or "memories." Decide at each step how thoroughly the students should read each portion of the text and insert the reading rate indicators accordingly. Be creative by making the map and journey as realistic and relevant as possible.

Implementing the guide

As with any new strategy, begin by explicating the purposes of the assignment to the students. Tell them that the map is designed to guide them through the reading by pointing out the most significant concepts and events. Next, have the students skim both the map and the coordinating text selections so they can "chart their course" and know where they are going before they get there. To further ensure understanding, work through the first few items as a class by modeling expected answers.

In the spirit of cooperative learning, students can be assigned a partner or choose someone with whom to work or "travel." They can take turns discussing their responses, reading and retelling portions of the text, and comparing the logic behind their chosen answers. As pairs of groups of students work on their guides, the teacher can circulate around the room to provide assistance and check on progress. Then, at selected points throughout the assignment, the teacher can engage the students in a class discussion of what has been completed so far.

Suggestions for optimal success

The following guidelines may be useful in the development and implementation of the Reading Road Map or any other reading or study guide.

1. *Build in a review of the content.*

As shown in the sample guide, (see question number eight) the students are asked to think back over specific topics from their reading. Such an activity forces a mental and/or written review of newly learned information, thereby enhancing comprehension and retention.

2. *Use creativity in designing the guide.*

Accompanied by a selection about Australia could be a guide in the shape of that country. A guide detailing voyages of the early explorers may be designed along the routes they followed. Similarly, in science, students may be led through a selection on arthropods by various sketches of millipedes, crustaceans or insects. Anything that deviates from the traditional dittoed sheet with questions is sure to arouse the interest of the most reluctant adolescent.

3. *Allow students to work together.*

Before explaining the guide, assign the students to groups or pairs or allow them to select a partner with whom to work. Preassigned arrangements can be determined on the basis of reading proficiency and subject area knowledge. In this way, students who may experience difficulty are grouped with those slightly more proficient so that all may contribute their varying degrees of expertise and benefit from the experience.

4. *Have students survey both the text and the guide.*

Teaching students to survey the new information in the text via the guide leads them on the way to effective independent studying. The survey step helps them to establish a mental set of expectations for the new content to be presented.

5. *Explain the purposes and model the procedures before beginning.*

It is essential that students understand that the purpose of a reading guide is to adjust their reading rate and help them focus on the most important information in the text. In addition, after explaining the purposes, work through several of the items as a class to ensure a thorough understanding of how the guide functions.

6. *Continually monitor student progress.*

As the class is working through the guide, the teacher should be circulating around the room to clarify points, answer questions, and monitor student progress.

7. *Be certain to include a discussion after completion.*

A reading guide should not simply be collected after its completion. On the contrary, it is an excellent vehicle to stimulate discussion and promote student to teacher interaction.

8. *Avoid assigning grades.*

Reading guides need not be graded in the traditional sense. As the name implies, their purpose is to serve as a guide not a test on the written material.

Consequently, a mark indicating completion or incompletion should be sufficient for grading purposes if anything is needed.

9. *Do not overuse the reading guide concept.*

The reading guide, like any new strategy, can lose its novelty if used too frequently with a class. It is best to choose chapters or selections which may be difficult for students to understand due to their heavy concept load or stylistic presentation.

10. *Help students become independent learners.*

The end goal of all instruction is to develop in students the skills and strategies necessary to learn from new material without teacher assistance. Students need to be shown how the strategies of selection, elaboration, and review learned and practiced via the reading guide can be applied to the reading of any material.

References

Armbruster, B. B. (1984). The problem of 'inconsiderate text.' In G. Duffy, R. Roehler & J. Mason (Eds.), *Comprehension instruction: Perspectives and suggestions.* New York, NY: Longman.

Armbruster, B. B., & Anderson, T.H. (1981). Content area textbooks. *Reading Education Report No. 23.* Champaign, IL: Center for the Study of Reading.

Cunnningham, D., & Shablak, S. (1975, Februar). Selective reading guide-o-rama: The content teacher's best friend. *Journal of Reading, 18,* pp. 380-82.

Davey, B. (1986, March). Using textbook activity guides to help students learn from textbooks. *Journal of Reading, 29,* pp. 489-94.

Educational Products Information Exchange (1977). *Report on national study of the nature and the quality of instructional materials most used by teachers and learners.* EPIE Report No. 17. Stonybrook, NY: EPIE Institute, 1977.

Goodlad, J.I. (1976). *Facing the future: Issues in education and schooling.* New York: McGraw Hill.

Herber, Harold L. (1970). *Teaching reading in content areas.* Englewood Cliffs, NJ: Prentice-Hall, Inc.

Singer, H., & Donlan, D. (1980). *Reading and learning from text.* Boston: Little, Brown and Company.

Vacca, R. T. (1981). *Content area reading.* Boston: Little, Brown and Company.

Wood, K.D. (1988). Guiding students through the reading of informational text. *The Reading Teacher, 41,* pp. 912-920.

How to improve comprehension through effective questioning

A strategy that focuses on the question-answer relationship helps students gain comprehension.

Socrates commented that "a good question is half the answer," and recent research has provided empirical evidence to support that notion. In fact, in 1983 Wixson found that when students are asked questions about the most significant information in a passage, they remembered the most significant information. When asked questions about the least important information (details and surface content), that was what they recalled. Similarly, Redfield and Rousseau (1981), after synthesizing the findings of many studies on questioning, concluded that student achievement is increased when teachers ask higher order questions, those questions which elicit critical and creative thinking. When lower order or literal level questions are asked students recall information verbatim with no real conceptual understanding of the content.

Unfortunately, studies have shown that teachers tend to ask the literal level type of question most frequently (Guszak, 1967). Studies have also shown that an overwhelming majority of the questions posed in textbooks, workbooks, texts, and manuals in the content areas are lower order or literal level (Tractenburg, 1974).

Numerous systems for classifying questions have been available in the professional literature throughout the years (Barrett, 1976; Bloom, 1956). All of these systems look exclusively at question type, categorizing them on the basis of whether they require lower or higher order thinking skills. A more recent system developed by Pearson and Johnson (1978) is more consistent with current views of how readers comprehend. Instead of merely looking at question type alone, this system looks at the interaction between the reader and the text. One of the criteria for classification is the question-answer relationship, that is where the reader must look to locate the information. Pearson and Johnson suggest that a three-way relationship exists between the question, the information in the text, and the preexisting knowledge of the reader. They suggest that a question can be classified as one of the following:

1. **Textually explicit.** The answer is explicitly stated in the text. It can be found "on the lines." An example would be:

Text: The farmer gazed at his empty thermos and started back.

TE Question: What object caught the farmer's gaze?

The answer, which is directly stated in the sentence, is the empty thermos. In other taxonomies, this would be called a literal level question, the kind which is most often asked by teachers. Notice, too, that such a question requires little thinking on the part of the student.

2. Textually implicit. The answer to this type of question is implied in the text. It can be inferred from the information provided but the answer is not directly stated. It can be found "between the lines." Sometimes these questions require that readers synthesize content from more than one sentence or paragraph. An example, again based on the text given previously, would be:

TI Question: Why did the farmer start back?

One of the answers implied is that he started back because his thermos was empty. The text does not explicitly state that he went back because of the empty thermos but that notion is suggested.

3. Scriptally implicit. The answer to a scriptally implicit question comes from the reader's background knowledge or prior experience (sometimes referred to as scriptal knowledge or scheme). In this case, the answer can be found "beyond the lines," or in the reader's head. Such questions require that the reader elaborate, embellish what is read by making inferences about the topic. In an oral discussion, in particular, an astute teacher might probe the students for more information by following the previous question with ones such as these:

SI questions:
   a. Why would an empty thermos make the farmer leave?
   b. What do you suppose was in the thermos?
   c. Where was the farmer before he left?
   d. Where did the farmer go?
   e. What are some other reasons the farmer might have left?

Notice how these questions require higher order thinking from the reader. None of this information is explicitly stated, instead students must fill in the gaps with the missing content. Since more than one answer is possible, it is important that the teacher adopt a very accepting, open demeanor, asking that students justify their responses when deemed necessary.

The QAR Program

Raphael and Pearson (1982) maintain that not only do teachers need training in how to ask effective questions but that students could benefit from training in how to find the sources of the answers. They developed the Question-Answer Relationship or QAR program to teach students strategies for answering questions. Corresponding with the three question taxonomy just presented, students can be taught three types of QARs. Notice how the terminology used in this training program is appropriate for students and how it helps them to distinguish among the sources for different answers.

Right There:
The answer is located on the page. It is on the lines. Words from the question and words from the answer are clearly stated in the book.

Think and Search:
The answer is harder to find. You might have to look in more than one sentence and piece the information together. It is "between the lines."

On My Own:
The answer is not found right in the book. You must find it in your head and use what you already know. The answer is "beyond the lines."

Researchers have had much success in training students of varied grade levels in how to distinguish question-answer relationships (Raphael, 1984; Raphael and Pearson, 1982; Wixson, 1983). Such training helps students become more aware of the task demands of questions and improves their answers. Based on this research, Raphael (1982) has suggested the following training model:

Step 1 - Introduce students to the QAR terms and concepts. Use one or two sentence examples (such as the "farmer" sentence shown) along with questions and answers from this category with the QARs already labeled. Discuss how each fits into the corresponding categories.

Step 2 - Again present students with a short passage with questions and answers but have them identify the QAR.

Step 3 - Give students the passages and questions and have them read and decide which of the QAR strategies is needed by writing their responses on paper.

Step 4 - Increase the length of the passage to approximately 75 to 100 words and increase the number of questions to five. Allow students to work through one passage as a class, then gradually release the responsibility to them in small groups, pairs, then individually; continually circulate among the groups to monitor student progress.

Step 5 - At this point, increase the passage to a full length text selection or story.

Step 6 - Generalize the strategies to other materials such as newspaper articles, films, and other subject areas (this is especially appropriate in the case of interdisciplinary teaming).

Good questioning is essential across the subject area. The following illustration shows how the system of classifying question-answer relationships can be applied to other areas such as science. If teachers in all subject areas become facile in the art of asking effective questions, and if students are shown the strategies needed to answer those questions, research and intuition clearly suggest that comprehension can be improved.

Science QARs

Text: A *solar eclipse* occurs when Earth moves into the moon's shadow. If Earth moves into the moon's umbra, a total solar eclipse occurs.

Right There or Textually Explicit
Q. What happens when the Earth moves into the moon's shadow?
A. A solar eclipse occurs.

Think and Search or Textually Implicit
Q. During a solar eclipse where is the moon in relationship to the Earth and the sun?
A. It is between the earth and the sun or in the moon's umbra or shadow.

On My Own or Scriptally Implicit.
Q. What is the environment like during a total solar eclipse?
A. It is dark and cold.
SI
Q. What do you suppose would happen to the earth if a total solar eclipse should remain for several months?
A. Numerous answers are possible here.

References

Barrett, T. (1976). Taxonomy of reading comprehension. In R. Smith & T. Barrett (Eds.) *Teaching reading in the middle grades.* Reading, MA. Addison-Wesley.

Bloom, B.S. (1956). *Taxonomy of educational objectives. The classification of educational goals. Handbook 1: Cognitive domain.* New York: David McKay.

Guszak, F.J. (1967). Teacher questions and levels of reading comprehension. In T.C. Barrett (Ed.) *The evaluation of children's reading achievement.* Newark, DE: International Reading Association.

Pearson, P.D., & Johnson, D.D. (1978). *Teaching reading comprehension.* New York: Holt, Rinehart, and Winston.

Raphael, T.E. (1982). Question-answering strategies for children. *The Reading Teacher, 26,* 186-190.

Raphael, T.E. (1984). Teaching learners about sources of information for answering comprehension questions. *Journal of Reading, 27,* 303-311.

Raphael, T.E. and Pearson, P.D. (1982). *The effect of metacognitive awareness training on children's question-answering behavior.* Technical Report #238. Urbana, IL: Center for the Study of Reading. University of Illinois.

Redfield, D.L. and Roussear, E.W. (1981). A metaanalysis of the experimental research on teacher questioning behavior. *Review of Educational Research, 51,* 237-245.

Tractenburg, D. (1974). Student tasks and test materials: What cognitive skills do they tap? *Peabody Journal of Education, 52,* 54-57.

Wixson, K. (1983). Questions about a text: What you ask about is what children learn. *The Reading Teacher, 37,* 287-293.

21

How to use brainstorming to improve comprehension

The Guided Reading Procedure is a simple way to help students remember much more of what they read.

We use whatever is stored in our minds, our prior knowledge, to make sense out of written (or spoken) material. Research on schema theory indicates that we all possess different "scripts," "associations," or, more appropriately, "schema" for concepts which are activated as we read. (Rumelhart and Ortony, 1977; Spiro, 1977; 1980). Since readers come to a printed page with different backgrounds of experiences, these variations determine how the text will be interpreted and what will be recalled (Anderson and Pichert, 1978; Carey, Harste and Smith, 1981). In a study by Anderson, Pichert and Shirey (1983), for example, it was found that asking subjects to read a passage from two different perspectives determined what they learned and remembered.

Because of their varied experiences, students quite naturally attached importance to different bits of information while reading and may not answer with the teacher's expected response. This may explain why it is often difficult to respond to a list of predetermined questions (usually prepared by the textbook author or the teacher) after reading. Students may have remembered quite a lot of information about the assignment but not specifically what the teacher wanted them to remember.

Teachers can capitalize on the varied backgrounds of their students by engaging them in associational thinking and responding (e.g. brainstorming) after reading. By using the "collective recalls" of the class as a whole, selected assignments can be greatly enriched.

The Guided Reading Procedure or GRP (Manzo, 1975; 1985) uses student input as a means of communicating the content of instructional material. After reading a segment of text, students are asked to recall whatever comes to their minds about the materials just read. The students engage in associational thinking as the responses of classmates trigger associations from their memories. In this way, since they can wait until a comfortable moment to respond, no one is put on the spot to answer a specific teacher-posed question. Then these "collective recalls" are written on the board in the order given and reorganized to coordinate with the text (e.g. in sequential order).

The GRP begins in the reading phase of the instructional lesson and extends through the post-reading phase. Therefore, it is essential that the teacher provide adequately for the pre-reading phase by building background knowledge, pre-teaching vocabulary, relating the new topic to the students' preexisting knowledge, and setting purposes for reading. Otherwise, the lesson would proceed by merely asking students to "open your books to page X and begin reading." Such a practice represents a serious departure from what is known about effective teaching and enhancing comprehension.

To implement the Guided Reading Procedure in the classroom, teachers can use or modify the following steps:

Step One: After the pre-reading introduction to the lesson, tell the students that their purpose is to read and remember all they can about the assigned selection. The selection is usually limited to no more the two to five pages of topically related information.

An option suggested by Manzo (1975) is to tell the students they have X minutes to complete the reading.

Step Two: With their books closed, ask the class to recall anything they can about the selection just read. Not being able to look back in the text forces students to actively retrieve the information from memory resulting in a mental or vocal recitation of the content.

Step Three: Write the "collective recalls" of the class on the board or on a transparency in the order given. Conclude this step when the class can no longer recall any more information or whenever it is deemed appropriate to move to the next step.

Step Four: Have the students skim the selection to determine if any significant information has been left out.

Step Five. The teacher and the class are now ready to reorganize the information given. It is recommended that the reorganization step follow the structure of the materials and may be in (a) sequential order as with narrative materials or events, (b) cause and effect, (c) comparison and contrast, (d) character analysis, or (e) main idea supporting details, to name a few.

Step Six: During the reorganization and afterwards, begin asking probing questions which will help students reflect on and make inferences about the content.

Step Seven: As an optional follow-up activity, give the students a test to determine their short term memory for the concepts discussed.

Manzo (1985) suggested that a metacognitive level of functioning be added to the GRP to help students become more aware of the learning processes and strategies used while reading (see Strategy 18 for a discussion of metacognition). This is accomplished by posing, at teachable moments, the question "What did you do to help you read and learn from today's lesson?" In this way, students are made aware of the self-correction strategies and the thought processes that best aid recall.

The illustration on page 100 depicts the collective recalls on a beginning lesson dealing with the Civil War in the east. Notice that, while the recalls are written initially in any order given, they are then reorganized topically under the two main battles discussed in the text. This sample lesson demonstrates the applicability of the GRP to expository text but it is extremely effective when used with narrative material as well.

A Final Note

The Guided Reading Procedure is appropriate for all subject areas and tasks including math word problems and following directions. Although described here in conjunction with reading, the steps can be applied to listening or viewing. The GRP is a favorite of teachers because it requires minimal preparation time.

However, the most outstanding feature of the Guided Reading Procedure is that through its use, all students, regardless of ability level, can make a contribution to the class with minimal risk. And since adolescents are particularly sensitive to taking social risks, it is rewarding to see them eager to contribute a word or phrase even when they are not called on to do so.

Abbreviated Lesson:
The Civil War in the East
1861-1864

I. The Collective Recalls of the Students

- Beauregard attacked Fort Sumter
- Jackson named "Stonewall"
- Battles have two names
- Bull Run
- Manassas
- Fort Sumter
- Creek named Bull Run
- Appalachian Mts.
- Poorly-trained volunteers
- No planning strategy
- April 12, 1861
- Union army under General McDowell
- Confederates confident
- McDowell attacked
- Beauregard 's forces

II. The Collective Reorganization of the Information

- Appalachian Mountains divided eastern and western wars
- No prepared strategy
- Poorly-trained volunteers

Fort Sumter
- Began April l2, 1861
- Beauregard and Confederates attacked Fort Sumter
- Charleston Harbor, S. C.

First Bull Run or Manassas
- Battles have two names:
- Confederates named them after settlements
- Northerners named them after bodies of water
- Creek named Bull Run
- Union army under General McDowell
- McDowell attacked Beauregard
- Jackson named "Stonewall"
- Union forces fled
- Confederates confident

References

Anderson, R. C., & Pichert, J.W. (1978, February). Recall of previously unrecalled information following a shift in perspective. *Journal of Verbal Learning and Verbal Behavior, 17,* pp. 1-12.

Anderson, R. C., Pichert, J.W., & Shirey, L.L. (1983, April). Effects of readers schema at different points in time. *Journal of Educational Psychology, 75,* pp. 271-79.

Carey, R. F., Harste, J.C., & Smith, S.L. (1981). Contextual constraints and discourse processes: A replication study. *Reading Research Quarterly, 16,.*(2), pp. 201-12.

Manzo, A. V. (1975, March). Expansion modules for the ReqQuest, CAT, GRP, and REAP reading/study procedures. *Journal of Reading, 28,* pp. 498-502.

Manzo, A. V. (1975, January). Guided reading procedure. *Journal of Reading, 18,* pp. 287-91.

Rumelhart, D. E., & Ortony, A. (1980). The representation of knowledge in memory. In Anderson, R.C., Spiro, R.J., & Montague, W.E. (Eds.), *Schooling and the acquisition of knowledge* . Hillsdale, NJ. Lawrence Erlbaum.

Spiro, R. J. (1977). Remembering information from text. The 'state of schema' approach. In *Schooling and the acquisition of knowledge.*

How changing perspective can improve students' understanding

Asking students to take on the point of view of a character in a selection can actually broaden their understanding.

The commonly heard cliche "put yourself in the other person's shoes" may have instructional as well as moral value. Studies have indicated that asking readers to change their perspective to coordinate with the content of the reading material can improve their comprehension and recall (Anderson & Pichert, 1978; Anderson, Pichert, & Shirey, 1983; Pichert & Anderson, 1977).

In one study, subjects were asked to read an ambiguous passage from different perspectives—a home buyer or a burglar. Those subjects who were told to read the passage as if they were home buyers learned information about the problems of owning a home. Those subjects told to read the passage as if they were burglars remembered information related to home security such as checking windows and doors, etc. Apparently, asking readers to change their perspective during reading activates specific dimensions of their prior knowledge, or schemata. Some of the reasons for the recall offered by the readers themselves included that changing perspectives (a) helped "jog" their memories, (b) made them pay attention to relevant details, and (c) caused them to fill in the gaps with information not explicitly stated. From these and other studies, it is hypothesized that giving an assigned perspective in advance of the reading causes readers to strategically focus on relevant

information, reconstruct this information, and make inferences while reading (Anderson & Pearson, 1984).

Point of view guides

One method for strategically leading students to broaden their perspective while in the act of reading subject area material is the Point of View Reading Guide (Wood, 1988). Like traditional reading or study guides, the point of view guide consists of a series of sequentially ordered questions to which students must respond during reading. Unlike the traditional guide, however, this guide requires that students change perspective and take on the point of view of the character, animal, plant, or object being studied. Students might read a portion of their social studies text as if they were Balboa discovering the eastern Pacific Ocean, their science text as if they were a volcano about to erupt, or their literature text as if they were Matilda in "The Necklace" or the madman in "The Tell-Tale Heart." Consequently, literary, historical, and scientific events become lifelike and dynamic for students, motivating them to want to read the assignment.

With the guide to lead them, readers essentially take on the schemata (the knowledge and experiences) of another individual. Or, simply stated, they must "get inside the head" of a character, trying to think, act, and feel from another's perspective. Because of the interview format, the guide questions elicit from the reader a combination of both text-based contributions (explicitly stated information), and reader-based contributions (information which comes from the reader's own prior knowledge). Thus, readers become personally involved with the content, enhancing their comprehension and recall.

Point of view guide questions differ from the questions typically asked of students in two ways. First of all, they are designed to be answered during the actual reading of the material. As such, they "divide" the reading material into manageable segments. In most textbooks, the questions are found at the end of the chapter and are frequently not presented in sequential order, making the reading and question answering task a difficult one for the majority of readers. The second difference is that point of view questions are in interview format and require a more elaborate response from the students. Below is an example which further illustrates this difference.

The guide on page 103 is for a chapter segment on the War of 1812. The initial statements develop readers' mental set by telling them that they are about to be interviewed as if they were a person living in the United States during the early 1800's. Notice how, throughout one lesson, the students become a merchant in a coastal town, a warhawk, a soldier under Captain Perry, two future presidents, a Cherokee Indian and a British soldier, to name a few.

While the guide covers several pages of text, the subsequent guide covers only two pages. Many subject area textbooks contain portions of text that present important concepts in a dense, overcrowded manner. Thus, in order to ensure adequate learning, the teacher may need to engage the students in a meaningful synthesis of the content. The guide on page 104 for a science lesson on "fungi" serves that purpose. In order to answer the interview questions, students can combine information from pictures, charts, diagrams, the text, and, most importantly, their own heads. The dialogue format is a welcome alternative to the rigid rhetoric commonly required by typical questions.

The last guide (page 105) represents a literature selection studied in language arts class. Instead of just reading about Kipling's *Rikki-Tikki-Tavi*, students actually become the mongoose and must respond to inquiring reporters in a telephone interview. Consequently, the reporter's first question is "What do you look like?" This gives students the opportunity to use their imaginations to embellish the main character. Subsequent questions enable the students to feel each of the experiences encountered along the way and to describe them from the first person.

Text Segment:
The propelling action of the paramecium's 17,000 hair-1ike cilia resembles a swimming stroke. The cilia do not all beat at the same time. A wave begins at one end and works toward the other end.

Traditional Question: What causes a paramecium to move?
Student Response: *The cilia*
Interview Question:
Your neighbors have complained about the ripples coming from your area. *How* can you justify these disturbances?
Student Response:
Well, with 17,000 feet like structures called cilia, it's hard to keep a low profile. Anyway, when my cilia start to move they look like "the wave" fans do at football games. Naturally, all this movement causes a few ripples here and there, but I'm hardly disturbing the peace.

Point of View Reading Guide
Chapter 11: The War of 1812
(Wood, 1988)

You are about to be interviewed as if you were a person living in the United States in the early 1800's. Describe your reactions to each of the following events.

Planting the Seeds of War (p. 285)
1. As a merchant in a coastal town, tell why your business is doing poorly.

The War Debate (p. 285-7)
2. Explain why you decided to become a war hawk. Who was your leader?
3. Tell why many of your fellow townspeople lowered their flags at half mast.
4. What was the reaction of Great Britain to you and your people at that time?
5. In your opinion, is America ready to fight? Explain why you feel this way.

Perry's Victory (p. 287)
6. In what ways were your predictions either correct or incorrect about America's willingness to fight this war?
7. Tell about your experiences under Captain Perry's command.

Death of Tecumseh (p. 288)
8. Mr. Harrison, describe what really happened near the Thames River in Canada.
9. What was Richard Johnson's role in that battle?
10. Now, what are your future plans?

Death of the Creek Confederacy (p. 288)
11. Explain how your people, the Cherokees, actually helped the United States.
12. Tell about your leader.

British Invasion (p. 288-90)
13. As a British soldier, what happened when you got to Washington, DC?
14. You headed to Fort McHenry after Washington; what was the outcome?
15. General Jackson, it's your turn. Tell about your army and how you defeated the British in New Orleans.

The Treaty of Ghent (p. 290)
16. We will end our interview with some final observations from the merchant questioned earlier. We will give you some names of people. Tell how they are now that the war is over: the British, the Indians, the United States, Harrison, Jackson.

Point of View Reading Guide
Topic: Science
Fungi

Imagine that you are fungi being interviewed by reporters for a television documentary. Write down in dialogue form your responses to their questions. Use your book as a guide.

p. 34 1 . Tell us about yourself and your family. How would we know you if we saw you somewhere?

Well, we're plant-like consumers, you know. In other words, we eat other things. We all have your basic cell wall and nucleus (our control centers). You've probably met our cousins—mold, mildew, yeast, and mushrooms.

p. 34 2. We hear you do a lot of good out there for man and the environment. Please, tell us how.

Gosh, well we're used in the food industry quite a bit. The mushrooms over there get fried and eaten with steak. Some of us look like mushrooms, but you wouldn't eat us, we're poisonous. Yeast causes bread to rise and is used to make vitamins. Some medicines are even made from our cousin, Penicillin.

p. 35 3. We also hear you have a negative side as well. Tell us about it.

Well, okay, okay. We'll tell. We mostly go after things made by other organisms like cotton, cloth or leather and we try to break them down. We even like plastic sometimes. We cause fruit to spoil and smell bad and bread to get moldy when it's left out. We don't like cool, dry places though.

p. 35 4. That's not all, what about your role in diseases?

All right, so we cause ringworm and athlete's foot. (That's a disease you can get in the locker room if you're not careful). We also go after plants and corn, causing corn smut.

Point of View Reading Guide
Topic: Literature
"Rikki-Tikki-Tavi" by Rudyard Kipling

Imagine that you are Rikki-Tikki-Tavi being interviewed by reporters over the telephone. Answer the following interview questions.

1. Since we are not there in person to see you ourselves, please, Mr. Tavi, tell us what you look like.

2. Mr. Tavi, how did you come to live with Teddy's family after all?

3. What was your first night in a strange place like?

4. How did you feel the first time you saw Nag? Describe Nag for us.

5. What was your reaction when you heard Nag and Nagaina plotting to kill the people you live with?

6. It must have been a very tense moment when you found Nagaina ready to strike at Teddy. How did you manage to divert her attention?

(Guides developed by Susie Avett)

Recommendations for use

To maximize success with the Point of View Guide, teachers will want to:

1. *Model and demonstrate.*

By the middle level years, students are very familiar with typical textbook-like questions and how to answer them. Encountering the interview questions introduced here will likely cause some confusion unless their purpose and use is explained in advance. The best approach is to give the class one or more sample responses either orally or graphically. Show them how such a response may require that they infer information from what was written in the text and fill in with some elaborations of their own.

2. *Group students.*

Consider allowing students to work in pairs or small groups to complete the guide. Make certain that the students are grouped heterogeneously so that all can benefit from the experience. Then, only one guide would need to be filled out between the pairs or small groups. To balance the responsibility, the role of recorder can be alternated with each question. Many times, working in groups reduces the risk of offering unusual responses on their own and permits students to "converge in their divergence," so to speak, in safe company.

3. *Praise creativity.*

Encourage creative responses through acceptance and praise. Any overt or implied criticism from the teacher or peers will instantly squelch students' imaginations. As they engage in their dialogues, have the students use written punctuation, interjections, cliches, stammering, or whatever realistically portrays the desired emotion.

Summary

The Point of View Guide is a strategy with many purposes. It engages students in a critical and creative thinking exercise and a writing activity while simultaneously helping them recall and assimilate new content. In addition, responding to expository or narrative material in the dialogue format required by the interview questions can be stimulating both affectively and cognitively. 🐴

References

Anderson, R.C., & Pearson, P.D. (1984). A schematheoretic view of basic processes in reading comprehension. In P.D. Pearson (Ed.), Handbook of reading research. New York: Longman.

Anderson, R.C., & Pichert, J.W. (1978). Recall of previously unrecallable information following a shift in perspective. *Journal of Verbal Learning and Verbal Behavior, 17,* 1-12.

Anderson, R.C., Pichert, J.W., & Shirey, L.L. (1983). Effects of the readers' schema at different points in time. *Journal of Educational Psychology, 75,* 271-279.

Pichert, J.W., & Anderson, R.C. (1977). Taking different perspectives on a story. *Journal of Educational Psychology, 69,* 309-315.

Wood, K.D. (1988). Guiding students through informational text. *The Reading Teacher, 41,* 912-920.

> Intelligence isn't so much what you know, rather, it is what to do when you don't know.
> —Elliot Eisner

How to improve critical thinking

A reaction guide is one means that can be used in all subjects to improve this important but neglected skill.

Researchers, educators, and psychologists have long proclaimed the need to teach students how to analyze critically and "think beyond the lines" when engaged in learning. The work of Robert Glaser (1984), amongst others, suggests that critical thinking should not be a separate entity but instead should be merged with the teaching of all subject areas.

Such an idea is a laudable one, but how can teachers develop critical thinking skills and simultaneously teach the subject matter of their classes. One way is through the use of an anticipation or reaction guide (Beall and Peterson, 1981, Readence, Bean, Baldwin, 1985), sometimes called a reasoning guide (Herber, 1970). The reaction guide is comprised of generalized, somewhat ambiguous statements on a topic to which students are asked to respond both before and after having read the related assignment. The result is a class of students who are engaged in active discussion and who have broadened their learning and/or changed their point of view in a motivating and socially rewarding manner. The reaction guide can be applied to a textbook chapter, unit or segment, or to a demonstration, class lecture, listening, or viewing assignment. The procedures for designing and implementing a reaction guide follow.

Designing the guide

Begin by analyzing the unit of study for its most significant concepts. Often it is beneficial to choose topics which reflect typical misconceptions (e.g. Astronomers believe that people's lives are controlled by the stars). Develop no more than ten statements presented in a general, thought-provoking manner (e.g. A statement such as "Rewards are a mixed blessing" is far more stimulating than "Everyone likes to be rewarded"). Include a column for responding both before and after the lesson. Another option is to include a column entitled "author" which allows the students to state the author's opinion to the statement by referring to relevant points from the text, lecture, film, or other information source.

Introducing the lesson

Distribute copies of the statements to the students and display one on an overhead projector, chalkboard, or poster paper. Arrange the students in pairs or small groups and tell them to take turns, reading each of the statements of their partners. The students do not have to agree with one another, but they must substantiate their responses. That is, they should explain to others, drawing upon personal opinion and experience, why they chose to agree or disagree with the statement. This is done to ensure that students do not rush through the assignment in true-false fashion thereby negating any possibility of discussion and sharing. The teacher should circulate to monitor the students' progress and help them to clarify their thinking.

Next, the teacher does an informal poll of class opinion by asking how many agreed or disagreed with each statement and tallying the number on the transparency. A non-judgmental posture will help to ensure that they feel comfortable with their divergent opinions.

After the discussion subsides, tell the students to read the selection on their own using the statements as their guides. As they encounter the concepts in the material, tell them to make mental or graphic notes of the new and relevant content. This portion of the lesson could even be done at home as well as in class.

The students then return to their groups and discuss each statement, responding in the "after" column. In many instances, their responses may not change although their knowledge of the content has broadened. The teacher then calls on the class to add their new knowledge to the concepts implied in the statements by elaborating and substantiating their responses. The students are required to present evidence from the lesson, for example, the textbook itself, which lends support for their answers.

One of the major advantages of the reaction guide is its applicability to all subject areas. This is particularly beneficial for teachers responsible for teaching more than one subject as in the case of blocked courses. Thus, it is a way for teachers to promote transfer of the skill of critical thinking to other contexts since research indicates that such transfer does not occur spontaneously (Belmont, Butterfield and Ferretti, 1982).

Examples of reaction guides from the four basic subjects of Science, English/language arts, Math, and Social Studies follow. All involve textbook material actually in use in middle level classrooms today. The directions for each reaction guide can be stated at the top of the page and should read something like: "Take turns reading each of the statements listed below with your partner(s). Then in the 'before' column, put a plus if you agree or a minus if you disagree with the statement. Be sure to substantiate your response with your partner(s) although you do not have to agree. After reading the lesson, put a plus or a minus in the 'after' column and talk through each answer with your partner(s) to see if you have broadened your view or changed your mind. Again, we will discuss these statements as a class so be certain to support your answers using portions from the text."

A reaction guide below is shown for a chapter segment on "Air" from a seventh grade earth science textbook. To emphasize significant concepts, the teacher may choose to develop a guide on a segment of a lesson.

Chapter 8 "Air"
Focus on Earth Science
Charles E. Merrill Publishing Co.

Before After

_____ _____ 1. The earth's atmosphere is made up of gases and liquids .

_____ _____ 2. Nitrogen is taken in directly as a food source for plants and animals.

_____ _____ 3. Without carbon dioxide, plants could not produce oxygen.

_____ _____ 4. The atmosphere is made up of two layers.

_____ _____ 5. The ozone layer keeps ultraviolet radiation from reaching the earth's surface.

_____ _____ 6. The coldest layer of the atmosphere is the stratosphere.

_____ _____ 7. Barometers measure the force and direction of air.

The guide below was used with a story on O.J. Simpson which appeared in a language arts anthology designed for remedial readers. (The author successfully used this guide to engage middle level students functioning below grade level in a lively, thought-provoking discussion both before and after the reading.)

Language Arts

Before   After

_____ _____ 1. If you are poor, chances are you will never be able to get very far.

_____ _____ 2. People who have been in a lot of trouble probably never change.

_____ _____ 3. Sometimes a person has to defend himself no matter what the cost.

_____ _____ 4. A mean attitude is necessary if you want to play good football.

_____ _____ 5. The ability to play a sport really well is something you are born with.

_____ _____ 6. You can do almost anything if you put your mind to it.

_____ _____ 7. People who are successful in sports are usually very lucky.

The third reaction guide is designed to assess and extend students' knowledge of factoring in an eighth grade mathematics class. Many guides, like the one shown, assume some prior knowledge on the topic and are an excellent way to review recently studied material. The fourth guide was developed for a sixth grade social studies lesson on "The Nile River Basin." Students' initial responses to number 5 dealing with the disastrous effects of flooding would rapidly change as they read of the advantages of flooding to farmers.

Mathematics
"Factoring Algebraic Equations"

Before   After

_____ _____ 1. The equation $2x^2$ is a quadratic equation.

_____ _____ 2. The equation x^2-2x+1 can be factored

_____ _____ 3. There is no solution to any equation that has a variable with a higher value than x.

_____ _____ 4. It is possible for $(2x + 4) \cdot (x + 4)$ to equal $x + 8$.

_____ _____ 5. The solutions to $2x^2-13x+15$ are $[+^3/_2 = 5]$

(special thanks to teacher, Jamie Wilhelm for contributing this reaction guide)

Social Studies
The Nile River Basin

Before   After

_____ _____ 1. The Nile River is one of the longest rivers in the world.

_____ _____ 2. Long ago the Nile was helpful in making the region around it prosperous.

_____ _____ 3. The Nile Runs through Morocco, Algeria, Libya, and Egypt.

_____ _____ 4. The presence of the Aswan Dam has been most beneficial to the people of Egypt.

_____ _____ 5. The flooding of the Nile River has always brought disaster to the people of the basin region.

_____ _____ 6. There is more than one Nile River in Africa.

References

Bean, T.W. and Pelerson, J. (1981) Reasoning guides fostering readiness in the content areas. *Reading Horizons, 21,* pp. 196-99.

Belmont, J.M., Butterfield, E.C., & Ferretti, R.P. (l982). To secure transfer of training instruct self-management skills. In D.K. Determan, & R.J. Sternberg (Eds.) *How much can intelligence be increased?* Norwood, NJ.: Ablex.

Glaser, R. (1984). Education and thinking: The role of knowledge. *American Psychologist, 39,* pp.93-104.

Herber, H.L. (1970). *Teaching reading in the content areas.* Englewood Cliffs, NJ: Prentice-Hall, Inc.

Readence, J.E., Bean, T.W., & Baldwin, R.S. (1985). *Content area reading: An integrated approach* (2nd edition). Dubuque, IA: Kendall-Hunt.

Six Principles of Learning as Described by Art Combs

1.**People learn best when they have a need to know.** This fact is basic, yet it is also overlooked. We expect students to need to know what we want to teach them — or if they don't, they should! Rarely do we make much effort to discover student needs and relate teaching to them. The genius of good teaching lies not in providing information but in helping students to discover needs to know they never had before.

2.**Learning is a deeply personal, affective experience.** Our brains are not switchboards or computers, but marvelous organs for the discovery of personal meaning, otherwise known as learning. The basic principle of learning from a perceptual orientation is this: Any information will affect a person's behavior only in the degree to which he or she discovers the personal meaning of information to the self. What is learned without personal meaning or feeling is unlikely to have much effect upon behavior.

3.**All behavior, including learning, involves self-concept.** What people believe about themselves affects their every behavior. The importance of the self-concept in human growth, learning, and health is one of the most significant discoveries of modern psychology. How people relate to any experience, including schooling, is inevitably determined in large part by what they believe about themselves. People who believe they can, try; people who don't, avoid the experience or defend themselves against it.

4.**Learning is governed by the experience of challenge or threat.** People feel challenged when they are confronted with problems of interest to them and which they believe they have a chance of coping with. They feel threatened by problems they do not feel able to handle. The experience of threat is destructive to most learning, while challenge enhances it. Whether students feel challenged or threatened lies not in the teacher's conceptions, but in the eye of the beholder.

5.**Feelings of being cared for and belonging have vital effects upon learning.** People who feel they are cared for and belong are likely to be excited, interested, motivated, want to get involved. People who feel rejected or alienated are likely to be turned off, discouraged, humiliated, disillusioned, apathetic and seek to escape from the scene or to attack the insiders.

6. **Effective learning requires feedback.** To be truly helpful, feedback should be: (a) immediate, (b) personal rather than comparative, (c) related directly to performance and should (d) point the way to next steps. Note that none of these are accomplished by the grading system.